Home Office Research Study 220

Religious discrimination in England and Wales

Paul Weller, Alice Feldman and Kingsley Purdam

with contributions from Ahmed Andrews, Anna Doswell, John Hinnells, Marie Parker-Jenkins, Sima Parmar and Michele Wolfe
of the University of Derby

"The views expressed in this report are those of the authors, not necessarily those of the Home Office (nor do they reflect Government policy)."

Home Office Research, Development and Statistics Directorate
February 2001

Home Office Research Studies

The Home Office Research Studies are reports on research undertaken by or on behalf of the Home Office. They cover the range of subjects for which the Home Secretary has responsibility. Other publications produced by the Research, Development and Statistics Directorate include Findings, Statistical Bulletins and Statistical Papers.

The Research, Development and Statistics Directorate

RDS is part of the Home Office. The Home Office's purpose is to build a safe, just and tolerant society in which the rights and responsibilities of individuals, families and communities are properly balanced and the protection and security of the public are maintained.

RDS is also a part of the Government Statistical Service (GSS). One of the GSS aims is to inform Parliament and the citizen about the state of the nation and provide a window on the work and performance of government, allowing the impact of government policies and actions to be assessed.

Therefore -

Research Development and Statistics Directorate exists to improve policy making, decision taking and practice in support of the Home Office purpose and aims, to provide the public and Parliament with information necessary for informed debate and to publish information for future use.

First published 2001

Application for reproduction should be made to the Communications and Development Unit, Room 201, Home Office, 50 Queen Anne's Gate, London SW1H 9AT.
ISSN   0072 6435

Acknowledgements

This report was written by Paul Weller, Alice Feldman and Kingsley Purdam, with additional contributions from Ahmed Andrews, Anna Doswell, John Hinnells, Marie Parker-Jenkins, Sima Parmar and Michele Wolfe. It is based on a postal questionnaire survey and local fieldwork conducted by Kingsley Purdam and Alice Feldman respectively.

The authors and contributors would like to thank all the individuals and organisations from the religious communities and public, private and voluntary sector bodies who participated in the research. We are grateful that individuals and groups from among these communities and organisations entrusted us with their experiences, stories, perceptions and views, whether by completing the project questionnaire or by taking part in local interviews. We would also like to acknowledge the contributions, both solicited and unsolicited, from a wide range of individuals as well as religious and other organisations at national, regional and local levels, which helped to inform the overall background to the project's work.

We have been conscious that in conducting this research, we have been dealing with matters that are of great importance in the lives of individuals, communities and organisations within the religious traditions of the country. We have also been aware of the potential significance and sensitivity of our research for local and national government, and for organisations in the public, private and voluntary sectors of the areas that we have been investigating. We have tried to conduct the research in ways that have been informed by an appropriate sense of accountability to our research subjects, to the commissioning agents of our research, and to the academic disciplines of our project team members.

We would also like to thank all others associated with the University of Derby who have contributed to various aspects of the research project as a whole. These include:

- Professor Ursula Sharma and Dr. Martin O'Brien who also have been part of the project team, contributing especially in the original planning and early months of the project

- Lynne Kinnerley, who worked as project secretary until the end of 1999

- Karen Rowlingson, who was involved in the early months of the project prior to taking up a new post at the University of Bath

- Louise Richards, the School of Education and Social Science Research Administrator with whose assistance the original proposals were put together

- Eileen Fry, the Project Manager of the University's MultiFaithNet Internet service, and Dr. Paul Trafford, its Internet Resource Developer until June 1999, who jointly prepared and maintained the project's website

- Jeremy Miles of the University's Institute of Behavioural Sciences who supported some of the statistical work of the project

- Viki Grant and Lisa Sheldon of the School of Education and Social Science Office who supported and facilitated project financial transactions

- Athiyah Ahmed, Matt Bateman and James Hatton, students of the University, who assisted in aspects of the project administration.

Finally, we would like to acknowledge the role of staff in the Research, Development and Statistics Directorate of the Home Office. In particular, this includes Jill Barelli and Kate Murray.

Acknowledgement is also due to other Home Office staff, past and present, including Marian FitzGerald and Joel Miller, who both played a role in the earlier stages of the project, and Philip Colligan and Neil Frater.

Professor Paul Weller (project director)
Dr Kingsley Purdam (research officer)
Dr Alice Feldman (research assistant)
Professor Marie Parker Jenkins (project associate director)
Professor John Hinnells
Ahmed Andrews
Anna Doswell
Sima Parmar (project secretary)
Michele Wolfe (project secretary and formerly research assistant to Professor Weller)

Contents

Summary

In recent years, individuals and organisations from a variety of religious traditions have begun to argue that discrimination exists on grounds of religion and that it deserves to be taken as seriously as discrimination on other grounds. Until now, however, there has been little research into the nature and extent of religious discrimination in this country.

In commissioning the research, the Home Office set the following objectives:

1. To assess the evidence of religious discrimination in England and Wales, both actual and perceived

2. To describe the patterns shown by this evidence, including:
   - its overall scale
   - the main victims
   - the main perpetrators
   - the main ways in which the discrimination manifests

3. To indicate the extent to which religious discrimination overlaps with racial discrimination.

4. To identify the broad range of policy options available for dealing with religious discrimination.

The specification for this report was that it should describe the findings of the research rather than offer extended analysis or recommendations. It is intended to inform debate and consideration of the policy options for tackling religious discrimination. A separate report, also commissioned by the Home Office, looks in more detail at the practical implications of some of these options for policy makers and legislators.

Methods

The findings are primarily based on interviews and discussions in four local areas and on a postal questionnaire survey of religious organisations.

For the local fieldwork, interviews and meetings were held in Blackburn, Cardiff, Leicester and the London Borough of Newham. There were 156 meetings altogether, involving a total of around 318 individuals, including representatives of religious organisations and representatives of secular agencies in the public, private and voluntary sectors.

The postal questionnaire was sent to 1,830 religious organisations throughout England and Wales, covering over 20 distinct faith groups. 628 questionnaires were returned, about two thirds from places of worship or meditation and the rest from national umbrella organisations, religious charities and community groups.

The scale and nature of religious discrimination

Ignorance and indifference towards religion were of widespread concern amongst research participants from all faith groups. This theme came up many times in the local interviews and was echoed in the postal survey. Ignorance and indifference do not in themselves constitute discrimination, but in organisational settings they can contribute towards an environment in which discrimination of all kinds (including 'unwitting' and institutional discrimination) is able to thrive.

In the local interviews, those who actively practised their religion often said that they were made to feel awkward and that they experienced pressure to conform. They claimed that other people based their views on pre-conceived ideas and stereotypes and seemed to neither know nor care about the things that are central to the experience of those for whom religious identity constitutes an important, or the key, aspect of their lives.

Hostility and violence were very real concerns for organisations representing Muslims, Sikhs and Hindus, although fear of violence did not seem to be a widespread issue in the local interviews.

In the postal survey, organisations that include a large number of people from visible minorities in their membership, particularly Muslims, frequently identified problems with organisational policy or practice as well as with the attitudes and behaviour of individuals. Christian organisations, on the other hand, tended to identify most of the unfairness experienced by their members with individual attitudes and behaviour.

Representatives from some of the religious traditions with a relatively small membership in this country were concerned that their very existence went unrecognised: sometimes because so little was known or taught about them; or because they felt themselves to be often misrepresented, or because they were being deliberately excluded. Such groups felt like 'minorities within minorities' who were being ignored by schools, employers, policy makers and service providers, even though these institutions may be working hard to include and involve the 'majority-minority' religions.

Is discrimination becoming more or less frequent?

Respondents to the postal survey were asked whether, in the last five years, problems such as ignorance, hostility and discriminatory practices had become more or less frequent.

- Muslim organisations were the most likely to say that the situation had worsened. The majority of Muslim respondents thought that hostility, verbal abuse and unfair media coverage had become more frequent. Views on organisational policy and practice were fairly evenly divided.
- Most Christian and Jewish respondents thought that things had stayed much the same, but a substantial number of Christians thought that ignorance, indifference and unfair media coverage had become more frequent.
- Some religious groups perceived improvements over the last five years. The majority of Buddhist and Bahá'í organisations, for example, said that ignorance was now less frequent.

Interviewees in the three English areas tended to feel that some progress was being made in reducing unfair treatment and that a degree of religious pluralism was beginning to develop, although much remained to be done. Quite a number of the interviewees in Wales thought that less progress had been made there and that it was still unclear whether devolution would promote or delay the process.

Who are the main victims of religious discrimination?

- A consistently higher level of unfair treatment was reported by Muslim organisations than by most other religious groups, both in terms of the proportion of respondents indicating that some unfair treatment was experienced, and by the proportion indicating that these experiences were frequent rather than occasional. The majority of Muslim organisations reported that their members experienced unfair treatment in every aspect of education, employment, housing, law and order, and in all the local government services covered in the questionnaire.

- Hindu, and especially Sikh, organisations also reported a relatively high level of unfair treatment and tended to highlight the same areas of concern as Muslim organisations.

- Christian organisations in the survey were generally much less likely to report unfair treatment than Muslims, Sikhs and Hindus, and nearly all the unfairness they reported was 'occasional' rather than frequent. However, black-led Christian organisations and those representing groups such as Mormons and Jehovah's Witnesses were much more likely to report unfair treatment in nearly all walks of life than organisations in what are often seen as the 'mainstream' Christian traditions. In the local interviews, such groups often described overt hostility similar to that experienced by some of the non-Christian minorities.

- Pagans and people from 'New Religious Movements' also complained of open hostility and discrimination, and of being labelled as 'child abusers' and 'cults', particularly by the media.

Who is responsible?

The research suggests that discrimination is much more likely to be experienced in some areas of life than others:

- Education, employment and the media were the areas most often highlighted in the postal survey and local interviews. The media were identified as the most frequent source of unfairness by people from all religious traditions.

- Traditions with a large membership of people from ethnic minorities (in particular, Muslims, Sikhs and Hindus) frequently reported unfair treatment in areas such as immigration, policing and prisons.

The postal survey gave some fairly consistent indications about the role played by the attitudes and behaviour of individuals compared with the policies and practices of organisations:

- In some areas of life (eg policing, prisons, immigration, health care, social services, transport) the attitudes and behaviour of staff employed by the service were seen by organisations from most religions as a more frequent source of unfair treatment than the policies of the organisations providing the service, although Muslim respondents, in particular, often felt that policies were at fault as well.

- In education and housing, pupils and neighbours or other tenants were often seen as the most likely source of unfair treatment. However, respondent organisations from some religions were equally likely to single out teachers.

- In employment, Christian and Jewish organisations were mainly concerned about the attitudes and behaviour of managers and colleagues, whereas other religions were also concerned about policy and practice.

- In the media, the attitudes and behaviour of journalists and presenters, and the coverage given to their religious community were both seen as relatively frequent sources of unfairness by respondents from all religions.

Is discrimination based on religion or on race and ethnicity?

Religions with large numbers of visible minorities, such as Muslims, Sikhs and Hindus, reported the most discrimination overall and research participants who belonged to these minority groups often identified a degree of overlap between religious and racial discrimination. Implicit or explicit references to racism were also common during the local interviews. Amongst Christians, black-led organisations were consistently more likely to say that their members experienced unfair treatment than Christian organisations generally. Many interviewees pointed to the artificiality of trying to separate religious and cultural identities.

However, there were also claims of unfair treatment from white people of British descent with no outward, visible signs of their religion. This suggests that such treatment can be a response to the nature of someone's beliefs and practices (for example, the hostility that is sometimes expressed towards groups that are often referred to as 'cults'). In other cases it may be the strength of belief and its effect on behaviour ("the more active you are, the more vulnerable you become") or the degree to which people seek to convert others. A number of interviewees pointed out that whilst there are those who see religion as an intrinsic or important part of their identity, the rest of society tends to think of religion as optional and may therefore assume that religious requirements can be negotiated.

Interviewees provided instances in which the rigid dividing line between religion and culture that is sometimes imposed by outsiders can prove awkward and divisive. For example, religious groups may have to present themselves as cultural groups in order to obtain local authority funding for the community services they provide. They feel uncomfortable about doing this, and people from religious organisations that are not associated with cultural minorities may feel discriminated against because they are unable to present themselves in this way.

What are the policy options?

Participants in the research favoured a comprehensive approach in which education, training, and a bigger effort to teach more about comparative religion in schools would all play an important part. This was in line with their repeatedly expressed views about the role of ignorance in fostering religious discrimination by individuals and by organisations in both the public and private sectors, and also with the view expressed in interviews that the media reinforce such ignorance and prejudicial attitudes.

There was scepticism about voluntary codes of practice because these often prove ineffective. Research participants recognised that the law has both strengths and limitations and did not think it would suffice on its own. However, some changes in the law might be needed in order to "send the right messages about discrimination". These could help if used judiciously and in conjunction with other approaches. The idea of legislation of some kind received most support from Muslim organisations and interviewees from ethnic minority groups.

In the local interviews, it was pointed out that the changes needed from employers and service providers were not necessarily expensive: quite small adaptations could be very helpful and sometimes it was as simple as trying to ensure that people were not made to feel awkward. There was a role for better guidelines and 'worked examples'. It was felt that employers and educationalists, in particular, could do more to accommodate religious diversity, and in a less grudging way.

In areas such as planning and funding, more 'mainstreaming' was required and greater acknowledgement of the services that religious organisations provide to their own – and sometimes to the wider – community.

Those from the less well known and the less 'mainstream' religions stressed the need for more inclusiveness – for example when holding events or carrying out consultation exercises.

Some interviewees, young as well as old, described a process of change and improvement to which they themselves had contributed. They suggested that religious communities could take some of the initiative themselves.

The project findings offer an evidence base in support of the conclusion of the Interim Report, published in January 2000, that it is "unlikely given the multifaceted nature and dimensions of unfair treatment on the basis of religion that any single response would be adequate or effective." The one previously identified option that the findings of the present report indicate would not be adequate to the described experience of unfair treatment and discrimination would be that of no new response. The Interim Report, which includes examples of possible policy options, is available on www.multifaithnet.org/projects/religdiscrim/reports.htm

1

Introduction

Background

In recent years, individuals and organisations from a variety of religious traditions have begun to argue that discrimination exists on grounds of religion and that it deserves to be taken as seriously as discrimination on other grounds. Until now, however, there has been little research into the nature and extent of religious discrimination in this country.

Some claims of unfair treatment have been made by groups who are also likely to suffer discrimination on grounds of race or ethnicity, making it difficult (perhaps unrealistic) to disentangle one form of discrimination from another. On the other hand, some of those claiming religious discrimination do not belong to an ethnic or racial minority, or they quote examples (eg Islamophobia[1] in the media) which do appear to be targeted more at religious belief and practice than at membership of an ethnic group or cultural tradition. The relative absence of law and policy that specifically recognises the possibility of religious discrimination has meant that people wanting to make formal claims of discrimination have had to rely where they can on other grounds (usually race or gender) even though they may feel that religion is the real basis of their claim.

This report describes the results of the primary research undertaken by this project. It provides a resource for government, for communities, and for organisations of various kinds in assessing the evidence about religious discrimination. An Interim Report from the research project was published in January 2000. This reviews the historical background, describes the current religious diversity of Britain, and provides information on anti-discrimination legislation in the UK and a number of other countries. It can be accessed via Derby University's *MultiFaithNet* website, which is to be found at http://www.multifaithnet.org

Objectives

In commissioning the research in April 1999, the Home Office set the following objectives:

1. To assess the evidence of religious discrimination in England and Wales, both actual and perceived

---

[1] Muslim organisations have been at the forefront in drawing attention to religious discrimination. Many of the concerns raised are discussed in *Islamophobia: a Challenge for Us All*, Runnymede Trust, 1997.

2. To describe the patterns shown by this evidence, including:
   - its overall scale
   - the main victims
   - the main perpetrators
   - the main ways in which the discrimination manifests

3. To indicate the extent to which religious discrimination overlaps with racial discrimination.

4. To identify the broad range of policy options available for dealing with religious discrimination.

The final objective could include legislative options as well as other measures such as policy reviews, voluntary codes of practice, or training and education programmes. However, the legal context has been much changed since the inception of the research project by the incorporation into British law of the Human Rights Act and the Treaty of Amsterdam, and is likely to change further as case law develops. The Home Office has therefore commissioned a separate report which looks at the legal options in more detail[2]. The present report simply indicates the extent to which research participants thought some form of legislative change might be useful.

Although the research concentrated on the views and experiences of people who identify themselves with a religion, this is not to ignore the possibility that secularists, humanists and agnostics may also experience discrimination on the basis of religion. Such experience also needs to be taken into account in framing policy in this area.

Research methods

The findings are primarily based on interviews and discussions in four local areas and on a postal questionnaire survey of religious organisations. However, they have also been informed by discussions and correspondence between the project team and a range of national organisations, religious and secular. In some cases the project team actively sought views from organisations that might not otherwise have made contact. In other cases this did not prove necessary as the organisations themselves took the initiative. In addition, a brief on-line questionnaire was placed on the project website, although in the event it was not widely used.

---

2 *Tackling religious discrimination: practical implications for policy makers and legislators*, Bob Hepple QC and Tufyal Choudhury, Home Office Research Study 221, 2001.

One point to bear in mind is that the reliance on religious organisations to answer questionnaires and participate in the local fieldwork will have tended to bring the research into contact with people who are actively practising their religion rather than those who may identify with a religion but be less devout or less involved in the organisational aspects. As was pointed out in the *Interim Report,* the active membership of many religions is much smaller than the number of people who identify with the religion in a broad sense. The views and experiences of these two groups may differ. For example, hostility and discrimination might be experienced more by the active membership – provided, that is, that they come into contact with secular agencies and with people from other religions or people with no religious beliefs.

A survey of individuals would ideally have been a much better option than a survey of organisations, but it would have been extremely difficult and expensive to obtain representative samples, especially of those religious groups with just a few thousand members. Even with the 'major' minority religions, it would currently be necessary to use information on ethnicity as a proxy in planning a sampling strategy and this is far from ideal[3].

Local fieldwork

Interviews and meetings were held in Blackburn, Cardiff, Leicester and the London Borough of Newham. The interviewees fell into three categories: individual members of religious traditions; representatives of religious organisations; and representatives of secular agencies in the public, private and voluntary sectors. Some of the representatives from religious organisations and secular agencies were seen in groups of two or more. There were 156 meetings altogether, involving a total of around 318 individuals.

The local interviews were more open-ended than the postal questionnaire described in the next section, and interviewees were not taken systematically through the same list of topics. Instead, they were asked about their own experiences as a member of a faith community, or as an employer, service provider, or advice worker as the case might be. The interviews with individual members of religious traditions were biographical in nature. The examples they gave of problems, difficulties and unfair treatment reflected the issues they wished to raise, and were not prompted by specific questions about employment, education and so on.

---

3   The 2001 Census in England and Wales will, for the first time, include a question on religion. People will be asked to choose from None, Christian, Buddhist, Hindu, Jewish, Muslim or Sikh, or to write in the name of any other religion. This will make it a little easier to plan surveys of individuals, since it will be possible to pinpoint geographical areas where there is a reasonable chance of finding representative samples of people from specific religions.

Religious individuals and organisations were also encouraged to give their views on how the problems they raised could be tackled. The secular agencies included employers, local authorities and the police. Such agencies have the potential to be both a source of discrimination, and to be a part of the solution. They were asked about their policy and practice in this area, their awareness of ongoing problems, and their views on how discrimination can be avoided or tackled. A range of organisations providing advice or community support were also interviewed. They provided an overview of the nature and extent of discrimination, and of the willingness and effectiveness of other agencies in dealing with the problem.

Questionnaire survey

The questionnaire at annex A was sent to religious organisations throughout England and Wales, covering over 20 distinct faith groups. These included Muslims, Hindus, Sikhs, Jews, Buddhists, Jains, Bahá'ís, Zoroastrians, inter-faith groups, 'New Religious Movements' (see glossary) and Pagans. Christian groups included Orthodox, black-led and Pentecostal churches as well as the Anglican, Roman Catholic and Non-Conformist traditions.

In designing the survey, the aim was to ensure where possible that each of these traditions was sent 50 questionnaires (in some cases more). With a target response rate of 60 per cent, this would have resulted in at least 30 completed questionnaires from each tradition. In a few cases (eg Jains and Zoroastrians) fewer than 50 organisations exist and the number of questionnaires despatched had to be reduced accordingly. In spite of the efforts described in annex B, the response rate from all traditions was lower than anticipated.

Sections C to J of the questionnaire have a very similar format. Each raises a particular topic (eg the policies of planning authorities or the attitudes and behaviour of police officers) and asks the respondent whether members of his or her organisation experience unfair treatment because of their religion. In each case the respondent could choose between frequent, occasional or no unfair treatment, or they could indicate that they did not have any experience in the area concerned. In addition, there was space on the questionnaire for people to write down specific examples of unfair treatment on the basis of religion, and to suggest ways in which the problem could be tackled. In describing results from these sections of the questionnaire, organisations that said they had no experience in the area concerned have been excluded from the analysis.

Some forms of unfair treatment or discrimination can be directed at religious organisations as well as their membership, or at the religion itself (an example of the latter might be media coverage). The precise wording of the questions was adjusted where appropriate to cover these possibilities.

The final section of the questionnaire asked respondents for their personal views on the seriousness of different forms of unfair treatment (eg ignorance, discriminatory policies, physical abuse); whether it was getting better or worse; the extent to which it might be based on racial hostility; and the measures that should be considered for tackling it.

A total of 628 completed or partially completed questionnaires were returned, representing an overall response rate of between 34 and 42 per cent (see annex B for an explanation of how this figure is derived and for a description of the measures taken to enhance the response). About two thirds of the responses came from places of worship or meditation, but replies were also received from national umbrella organisations, religious charities and community groups of various kinds.

The results from the survey need to be treated with caution for a number of reasons.

- The low overall response raises the possibility that the results will be biased. For example, organisations that do not think religious discrimination is a particular problem may have been less likely to reply, thus biasing the results towards those who do. The language and style of the questions may not have been very accessible to people from some cultural traditions.

- The representative from each organisation who completed the questionnaire was set the difficult task of trying to reflect the collective experience of his or her membership. Organisations are likely to vary in the extent to which they have good records or direct knowledge on which to base these judgements. Feedback to the research team indicated that some organisations consulted with their membership before responding.

- The number of organisations responding from within each religious tradition was further reduced for the purpose of analysis because respondents could bypass questions or topics on which they had little or no experience. This means that the reported experience of some traditions is sometimes based on a handful of responses. Percentages based on such small numbers are unreliable and have not therefore been used in this report.

- The ratio of national to local organisations in the survey varied considerably between religions (see annex B). In most religions, both types of organisation gave similar responses. However, it should be noted that national Muslim organisations were consistently more likely to indicate that their members received unfair treatment than local Muslim organisations. 56 per cent of the total Muslim responses came from national organisations.

Thus the questionnaire survey does not provide precise statistical data. However, it does give a reasonable impression of the views within each tradition and of the areas of public life that cause most concern to religious groups. The results generally tally reasonably well with the findings from the qualitative interviews.

The methods used in the research and the response rates are described in more detail in the technical report at annex B. Table 1.1 below gives the total number of questionnaires returned from each religious tradition. However, as mentioned above, the number of organisations answering a particular question may be much less than this.

Table 1.1 Number of questionnaires returned by each tradition

Minority traditions		Christian traditions	
Bahá'í	25	Anglican	27
Buddhist	33	Baptist	24
Chinese	7	Black-led	15
Hindu	37	Ecumenical	27
Inter-faith	27	Independent	25
Jain	7	Methodist	27
Jewish	40	New Church	21
Muslim	70	Orthodox	9
NRM*	11	Pentecostal	23
Pagan	12	Presbyterian	6
Sikh	35	Roman Catholic	20
Zoroastrian	7	National organisations**	33
Other	6	Other***	54

* New Religious Movement (see glossary)
** National Christian organisations were not allocated to specific traditions when analysing the summary data
*** Mainly comprising Church of Christ Scientist, Jehovah's Witnesses, Unificationists, Church of Jesus Christ of Latter-day Saints

Clearly, organisations from some religious minorities are represented to a much greater extent in the survey results compared with their numbers in the population. In presenting the findings, it would be erroneous to quote overall totals for all religions without 're-weighting' the results. This has not been done, because without the kind of basis that Census data would provide, there is no reliable way of knowing whether the number of organisations in a particular religion is an accurate reflection of the number of adherents. Instead, the findings for each religion are presented separately.

In this report the responses from the Christian traditions have often been combined for the sake of simplicity, although the sample was designed so as to emphasise the full range of such traditions and was not therefore statistically representative (if organisations had been selected according to numbers in the sample frame, most would have been Anglican or Methodist). However, most of the individual traditions responded to questions in a similar way, and the text draws attention to any exceptions. These mainly involved organisations in the black-led and 'Christian (other)' categories, both of whom were generally more likely to report unfair treatment than other Christian traditions.

Terminology

There is a glossary at the end of the report covering the terms used by research participants (eg relating to religious festivals or items of clothing).

Throughout the report, 'interviewees' refers to people who participated in face to face meetings with the researchers in one of the four local areas, whilst 'respondents' refers to people who completed postal questionnaires. It is important to remember, however, that for the vast majority of questions, respondents were completing the questionnaire on behalf of an organisation. They were asked not about their individual experience of unfair treatment, but about the experience of their membership or, where appropriate, the experience of the organisation itself.

The questionnaire deliberately referred to 'unfair treatment' in order to be as inclusive as possible and to capture any sort of grievance. As will be seen from responses to the survey, and from the local interviews, such treatment can range from a violent assault to a chance remark that unwittingly conveys a pre-conceived idea or stereotype.

Where the term 'discrimination' occurs in this report, its use is analogous to discrimination based on race, gender or disability. This might mean, for example, treating someone less favourably because of their religious belief, identity or practice (direct discrimination); disadvantaging a whole group of people because unnecessary rules or conditions are imposed that can be met by more people from one religion than another (indirect discrimination); or the collective failure of an organisation to provide an appropriate and professional service to people because of their religion (institutional discrimination). It might also include failing to make the kind of 'reasonable accommodation' that would enable someone from a religious minority to take up a job or make use of a service.

When considering religious issues, there is a further dimension which the Interim Report for this project termed 'religious disadvantage'. This refers to certain historical privileges afforded to the Church of England which are not available to non-Established religions and which can be seen, for example, in the provisions made for religious chaplaincy services in public institutions such as the NHS.

Clearly, not all unfair treatment constitutes discrimination. People may feel hurt by the views – or the ignorance – of others with whom they come into contact, without the latter having done anything that is unlawful or discriminatory. At the same time, actual discrimination may occur in the absence of individual prejudicial views or attitudes.

Structure of the report

Religious, ethnic and cultural identities can overlap in ways that make it difficult to know which type of identity is being targeted by those responsible for hostility, prejudice or discrimination. Chapter 2 examines the views of interviewees and respondents on this issue.

Chapters 3 to 10 each deal with a particular area of life (employment, education and so on). Findings from the questionnaire survey are presented first, along with specific examples of discrimination that were provided by respondents. This is followed by the experiences described in local interviews. Most of these chapters also have a final section which looks at the range of solutions proposed by research participants.

Chapters 11 and 12 deal respectively with unfair treatment of one religious group by another, and the role of political and pressure groups.

Chapter 13 gives the overall views of research participants about the nature and extent of unfair treatment, and whether it is getting better or worse. This chapter also reviews the earlier findings in the light of the research objectives and poses some overarching questions:

for example, is more discrimination and exclusion caused by the attitudes and behaviour of individuals, or by the collective failings of organisations? Did research participants detect a gap between the policies and practices of service providers? Is discrimination real or perceived, and is it based on religion, ethnicity, or a mixture of both?

The final chapter presents the views of research participants about the way forward.

Annex C provides data from the questionnaire survey. As noted earlier, the small number of respondents from some religious groups does not make it practical to provide charts and percentages. On the other hand, extensive use of actual numbers would soon make the text difficult to read and unwieldy. Annex C therefore provides the detailed evidence for points made throughout the report. It can be examined further by anyone interested in the findings for a particular religious tradition or for a particular area of life in which discrimination may occur.

The results are presented in a condensed form which should make it easier to compare religious traditions and topics, as well as saving space. In part 1 (which covers the topics in chapters 3 to 10) the combined results from Christian respondents are shown for ease of comparison with other faith groups. Part 2 gives the results for individual Christian traditions.

You are instantly more vulnerable if you wear traditional dress, whether you wear it for religious or cultural reasons
(a Muslim interviewee)

It is not always clear whether people who demonstrate hostility to those with some outward sign of 'otherness' such as skin colour, language, or dress have feelings against a particular religion in mind. Claims of unfair treatment on the basis of religion are often made by groups that include a substantial proportion of people who also suffer discrimination on the basis of ethnicity. However, such claims are also made by converts who do not share the ethnicity of most of their co-religionists, and by people from New Religious Movements and Pagans, the majority of whom do not belong to ethnic minorities. A high proportion of cases to do with religion that have been to the European Court of Human Rights relate to the latter.

Religion and ethnicity are highly complex. They are both difficult to define, and yet both shape people's experiences and form part of their identity. Inevitably, the relationship between them is even more complicated and contested. This chapter starts with the outcome of the postal survey question on this issue, although the complexity of people's actual experience is perhaps reflected more fully in the subsequent section, where interviewees describe the situation for themselves.

Findings from the questionnaire survey

Some religious people, as a matter of principle, make no distinction between their religion and their ethnicity or race. Others have a strong wish to do so, even when (as can happen in England in Wales) religion and ethnicity are closely aligned.

Having answered questions about the potential areas of discrimination that are described later in this report, respondents from religious organisations were asked to say how far ethnic or racial grounds formed part of the reason for unfair treatment on the basis of religion. The answers, given in table 2.1 below, suggest that people representing religions with a high proportion of ethnic minority members see a clear area of overlap between religious and racial discrimination.

Table 2.1 How far do you think that in your religion, ethnic or racial grounds are part of the reason for unfair treatment on the basis of religion?

	Not part of the reason	A small part	A large part	The main reason	Don't know	Total
Bahá'í	8	6	3	2	4	23
Buddhist	14	2	5	4	4	29
Christian - black-led	0	3	5	2	3	13
Christian – all other	165	46	19	5	29	264
Hindu	4	9	8	8	3	32
Jain	1	3	0	0	1	5
Jewish	5	9	8	7	6	35
Muslim	4	20	22	11	4	61
NRM/Pagan	20	0	2	1	1	24
Sikh	0	9	12	10	3	34
Zoroastrian	1	2	0	2	0	5

All Sikh and a large majority of Muslim and Hindu respondents felt that ethnicity played at least some role. Most Jewish respondents felt the same, although opinions were more evenly divided. In contrast, nearly all the NRM/Pagan organisations felt that ethnic or racial grounds played no role at all.

Some Christian Churches have mixed or predominately black congregations, and some forms of Christianity are specifically associated with African or African Caribbean traditions. It is perhaps not surprising, therefore, that a significant minority of Christian respondents (around one in three overall) felt that ethnic or racial grounds formed at least some part of the reason for discrimination. However, only the black-led Christian organisations were as likely as Sikhs, Muslims, Jews and Hindus to say that ethnicity or race was a large part of, or the main, reason for discrimination. From the comments reproduced below, it seems that respondents from black-led groups often had other Christians in mind when thinking about the role of racial discrimination.

National and local organisations within each religion gave broadly similar views. However, ethnicity tended to play less of a role in the view of national Muslim organisations than in the view of local organisations.

The number of respondents answering 'don't know' to this question may also be significant. The interviews discussed in the next section and the comments from questionnaires reproduced below suggest that people who experience unfair treatment do not always find it easy to pigeonhole discrimination into one category or the other, and may sometimes come up with contradictory views.

The relationship between unfair treatment on grounds of religion and on grounds of ethnicity – quotes from the postal survey

Bahá'ís: *"there is an ingrained suspicion of any coloured group"*, *"it is a mistake to mix ethnic, race and religion issues"*, *"it is ethnic discrimination for some things and religious discrimination for others"*

Buddhists: *"fear of unknown"*, *"race is irrelevant – they see us as devil worshippers"*, *"only Asian Buddhists, not white Buddhists, who suffer discrimination"*

Christians: *"race is a factor"*, *"secular governments would love to ethnicise religious groups"*, *"bias of government towards minorities"*, *"there are different dynamics at work for minorities and whites"*, *"problems because origin of faith is overseas"*, *"ethnic and racial discrimination is not connected to religious discrimination"*

Black-led Christian traditions: *"there is no racial equality in the church"*, *"non-white members experience difficulties"*, *"suspicion between black and white Christians"*, *"black-led Churches seen as hindering church progress"*, *"people made to feel unwelcome and unwanted"*, *"black fundamentalist Christians faced with hostility"*

Hindus: *"ignorance and assumptions are made on racial grounds"*, *"religion is used as social and political tool for unfair treatment"*, *"no tolerance from other religious groups"*

Jews: *"historical anti-Semitism has not diminished"*, *"wrong assumptions about Jews"*

Muslims: *"suffer from colour, racial, ethnic, and religious discrimination"*, *"discrimination because of colour/origin and religion"*, *"ignorance is the main cause"*, *"in some physical incidents race and religion are linked"*, *"racists cannot analyse between race and religion"*

NRM/Pagans: *"Pagans get vilified"*, *"the perception is that we should be Christians"*

Sikhs: *"[prohibited from] wearing the Kirpan at airports'"* *"dress, beard and turban"*, *"ridicule of children due to long hair and police racism"*

Zoroastrians: *"unfair treatment occurs as a result of race"*, *'"racial prejudice arises from ignorance"*

Local interviews

In the face to face interviews, people expressed their religious identification in a variety of ways. But, in the main, this identity was seen as being intimately linked with other aspects of who they – and others – see themselves to be.

Visible difference and identity

The ethnic, cultural and religious aspects of individuals' identities are often closely related and visibly apparent. The response to this 'visible difference' may lead to an intensification of unfair treatment:

> If you're a Hindu, you have problems. If you're a Hindu with a dot, you have more problems.

One man observed that his wife, who has converted to Islam, seemed to experience less unfair treatment than other Muslim women who are ethnically different from the majority society. As another, Muslim, interviewee put it:

> You are instantly more vulnerable if you wear traditional dress, whether you wear it for religious or cultural reasons.

A Muslim woman explained that things are especially difficult for women:

> Women have always had it rough, white or Asian. If you're Asian and a woman, it's worse. If you're Asian, female and Muslim, it's worse still.

But despite the problems incurred as a result of the responses to such visible markers of difference, a Sikh educationalist observed that:

> You have to let people know; you have to be strong enough not to conform - like cut your hair in order to be accepted.

He recalled applying for a job over the telephone, and when he showed up for interview, the woman interviewer was: "gob smacked – she was so surprised that people could look so different but have the same speech". He felt that:

... positive action is needed so people are encouraged to be accepted. Despite looking different, they have the same core values.

Interviewees who were members of minority ethnic groups often felt that in practice religious and racial discrimination were not separable. Many emphasised that unless one has been a victim of discrimination, one cannot really know whether something that has occurred is based on race or religion. Where religious identities, beliefs and practices are closely linked to an individual's cultural, ethnic and national background, negative responses and unfair treatment based upon their identities and traditions may also be related to expressions of racism and xenophobia. A female African-Caribbean race equality worker observed that:

Harassment due to religious difference might be part of an overall racist perspective. If a person is or has been targeted, the perpetrator will target all their 'weaknesses' or vulnerabilities for attack.

However, for some people, religious identity is the foremost aspect and expression of who they are. They may identify clear differences between racial and religious discrimination. This is especially so when, as in the case of female Muslims and male Sikhs, the visible expressions that distinguish them as different are religious.

Other ways of being different

Religious difference, however, is not solely a matter of visible difference, nor is discrimination on the basis of religion limited to racism. A member of an Evangelical Christian group observed that:

... the more active you are the more vulnerable you become.

A member of the Church of the Jesus Christ of Latter-day Saints stated:

After a while, over the years, so many people have had to live a secret existence...I can't share my religion without being in a watertight relationship, and even that doesn't always work.

Difference, and the desire to maintain it, can often be seen as problematic in itself. An Orthodox Jewish man explained that being different is not well-understood, and that the desire to be different can often be misinterpreted for something else:

While I don't want my own daughter to marry outside the religion, and while I might teach her to look for a Jewish husband, I don't teach her to hate others. I believe people don't know how to deal with or understand the difference between the two.

At the same time, a member of the Progressive Jewish tradition noted that Jews are targeted whether or not they are observant, because they are perceived as being Jewish even if they don't identify themselves as such. He added that Hasidic Jews are seen as 'weird' and that is then further attributed to all Jews. At the same time, one active member of the Orthodox Jewish tradition stated that he did not think that non-Jewish people know what Judaism is. He felt that *"There will be discrimination for people who are different"*. He also believed that such discrimination will last for at least a generation. However, in respect of particular localities, he also attributed this to *"resentment of new people coming to an area rather than the fact that they are different or Jewish"*.

Interviewees reported problems stemming from being identified as a 'foreigner' or from being associated with what is regarded as a 'foreign religion', no matter what the ethnic background of the individual concerned. For example, a member of the Church of Jesus Christ of Latter-day Saints reported that members of his Church:

...are seen as different from whites because they are seen as Americans, despite attempts to explain the founders of the Church of Jesus Christ of Latter-day Saints came from here...people in this part of the country are quite insular; they don't like change; they don't like things of a foreign nature – that's "not of our country or area"...

A Roman Catholic Christian representative noted that in modern Welsh, terminology is used that is associated with the notion of 'papist' and that this tends to denote 'foreigner'. He saw this as feeding into a prejudicial and continuing rhetoric that Catholics are not really loyal to the state. Drawing attention to the fact that the mainstream 'white' society is not homogenous, another Catholic who goes to a large, culturally diverse church (including people of Irish, Polish and other backgrounds) highlighted issues of class stating that, in Wales, *"there are not a lot of poor people going to Anglican/Methodist churches"*.

Understanding religious identity

Most respondents emphasised the complexity of the relationships between ethnicity and religious identity. For example, when discussing the things that make people feel Jewish, a group of Jewish discussants identified an array of things from culture and ethnicity, to philosophical, religious and theological beliefs. For many, it was just a *"feeling"* they had, whether they had been born into the religion or had adopted it. While the identity of some was closely linked to religious study (especially for those in the process of converting), for others it was simply *"all they had ever known"*, and was thus an unavoidable part of themselves.

Christians of minority ethnic backgrounds often reported being subject to external expectations connected with the relationship between religion and ethnicity. In many ways they felt that such expectations restricted their identities. For example, two African-Caribbean women, one a Roman Catholic and one an Anglican, noted that because of their colour, other people always seemed to assume that they were members of a 'black-led' Church since, *"There is an assumption that race identifies faith"*. Another Christian stated that he did not want to be labelled as an *"Asian Christian"*. Rather than being categorised in this way he would like *"to be part of the whole Christian family"*. He complained that:

> People always say 'ethnic, ethnic', but what about us as Christians?

The complexity of religious identity and difference carries over into attempts to define and respond to religious discrimination. A Muslim woman observed that:

> If someone throws two stones through someone's window, that's racism. If they throw two pigs heads [as did happen in this person's experience], it's about religion.

However, as a male African-Caribbean race equality worker observed when this story was recalled:

> I don't care what they threw, but why they threw anything at all – the whole gambit of 'ifs'. You're usually dealing with a multiplicity of issues.

Another echoed this perspective, stating that he felt people would always find a reason to discriminate or to stratify others. At the same time, other interviewees were concerned that an emphasis on their religious identity might further restrict the ways in which others see them. A person with both African-Caribbean and Asian family origins in Trinidad stated that he felt people would always find a reason to discriminate against and/or to pigeonhole others, remarking that:

> People don't know I'm Catholic – they see me as Asian, hear my accent and think I'm Caribbean – they already have enough pigeon holes to slot me into. I haven't had the occasion to tell them about my religion!

He added that the issue is much bigger than what religion a person is, and that it:

> ... relates to a larger social ill rather than a religious issue. I couldn't care less what religion people are, but about what affects peoples' lives and to put those things right regardless of any particular attributes.

A youth worker attempted to bridge the various dimensions and tensions involved in this issue involved by proposing that:

> ...if you use the term 'cultural discrimination', and look more holistically at the issues, you can begin to approach the issue in terms of whether the communities' needs and cultural aspirations are being met, rather than trying to determine whether it is racial or religious discrimination or determining what discrimination is, and categorising the problems people have...

Whether or not individuals and groups feel that religion is a or the key issue that needs to be addressed, a female African-American race equality worker emphasised that a problem remains with regard to the perceptions of the wider society because:

> ...religion is often not seen as intrinsic to identity as opposed to the case where race is.

She observed that in a society which can be seen as increasingly secular, it is almost expected that one must 'negotiate' one's religious identity – that it can somehow be bargained or traded off, or that people can choose to live without it. She felt this leads to "a situation where people are actually saying we're not asking you to change who you are but just what you do at certain times". In contrast with the assumption behind such an approach, she felt that:

> ... dealing with religious issues may actually get deeper than race because it goes across the board and touches all communities. It could act as a very good bridge because it cuts across the whole continuum of identity, including people who do/don't want to be seen as different – and everything in-between.

Young peoples' religious and ethnic identities

Some previous research has argued that the identities of young people within minority ethnic communities are more hybrid than those of their parents and grandparents. Arguments have also been put forward to suggest that the role of religion will diminish in coming generations, especially within ethnic minority communities. This part of the chapter therefore includes information provided by young people during the course of interviews with other family members, as well as material derived from three group interviews with young people in the setting of a community centre and extra-curricular groups.

One religiously and culturally mixed group of young girls was more concerned about gender inequality in the ways that teachers treated them in comparison with the boys in their classroom. For others, experiences of racism which might have been common during their early school years seemed to dissipate by the time they reached their early teens. One Zoroastrian youth observed that, in his particular experience, racism in terms of being called 'Paki' faded out by year seven. He attributed this mostly to stricter sanctions on racist language and behaviour and also to students now learning more about ethnic minorities. He said his friends and those of his siblings are now "*all right about who we are*" because, through friendship, they have learned more about Zoroastrianism and it was no longer a big issue.

A white, male, Welsh youth worker noted that young people in their late teens seem to be at the age where they are "*looking for a cause*" and that, typically, they may become interested in religion in their early twenties. A Jehovah's Witness parent explained some of the dynamics involved in this:

Adolescence adds issues and complexities on top of this, so you end up with the God issue plus standing apart from your peers, at a time when these issues come up regarding experimenting with drugs and alcohol. If it is a matter of faith, then teens may end up questioning their faith, and a lot of Jehovah's Witnesses would go through a lot of questioning as they are often desperate to belong, and to be outside your peer group because of religion, well you really have to believe. So you have this questioning phase on top of taking a lot of grief and questions from peers etc. It's a time of a crisis of conscience. Once they leave school however, they then move into new peer groups and can re-establish themselves. But the last couple of years of school are very tough, and we often lose many young people; yet there is an ebb and flow in that we may lose them at this time, but they come back in their twenties.

A Sikh educationalist noted that:

…youngsters may be conforming to conventional traditional norms, but underneath, they are having their own identity: 'I'm a Christian, I'm a Sikh, a Hindu - whether I go to Church or not, I feel pride'.

A male, African-Caribbean, youth worker pointed out that:

They have a bit more freedom, but it only takes one event to divide people.

In respect of such young people, an Asian, male, representative of Student Services noted that:

Religion has become a scapegoat. The Rushdie Affair was about young people's anger, about being unhappy with their lives. Such campaigns get overtaken by the bandwagon. Young people are now more educated than their parents and think they know more than their parents do – they focus on intellectual arguments, whereas older people are of the philosophy, 'we can carry on living in this society if we can build mosques (which is itself an achievement) and have halal grocers'.

Having noted the perspective of the young people, however, he went on to ask:

...what have the kids done yet? Their parents fought for their kids' right to eat halal meat at school, eating with their hands, wearing the dot....

Nevertheless, some young people do see themselves in a position of being able to speak out on behalf of their elders who could not, or would not do so on their own behalf. A Jewish man observed that Jewish communities have either gone the way of complete assimilation or of separation. He noted that his parents' generation would not have talked about these issues, but that now his generation are doing so and they are trying to bridge the gaps. A young Sikh man remarked that:

You can't appreciate racism unless you've experienced it. I was born here. My great granddad fought for this country. I demand my rights whereas my Mum accepts the whole situation.

He explained that he could tell hundreds of stories of racism about the place where he and his brother work and that because of such racism, he is becoming increasingly cynical towards society. He pointed out that he had *"become westernised a few years ago"* but that now, in the face of such poor treatment, he is becoming more politicised about his culture and identity. But, according to an Asian, male, rights worker, when young people seek out alternative avenues of belonging:

... the people along those ways are only conservative – there are no progressive organisations and interpretations.

In response to this, the rights worker says that his approach is to try to emphasise that:

Yes, you can be proud of being Muslim, but remember the importance of university, etc. Wear a turban, but remember Guru Nanak's best friend was a Muslim, and saw it as a 'we'.

He felt that there was increasing evidence that things are moving into a phase in which:

...there will be progressive elements from the Muslim community emerging, and who will challenge the conservative perspectives.

At the same time, he believed that there was also a need for progressive 'secular' political spaces that could serve as a point of interaction for the political and religious components of communities, even though many people feel that it is not possible for these to be brought together. He concluded that:

We must get to the point where the secular framework doesn't mean we are anti-religious. We must construct a framework that allows you to be, and still establish a framework that we can all be part of.

why can't they chop off that bun?!
(a Hindu educationalist reporting comments by teachers who had, in this way,
derided Sikh children and their hair)

The formal education system directly impacts upon the lives of almost the whole of the population. It is, at least potentially, a lifelong means to individual achievement, personal growth and the expansion of economic opportunity. It is also – and especially in respect of the school system – an arena within which family traditions and identities come into interaction with the beliefs and values of the wider and more diverse society. Such interaction can result in significant tensions for parents, children, and teachers alike. These tensions can either take the form of conflict or of negotiation.

The education system is also important because it can be the means by which attitudes and values are initially formed and, later, critically evaluated. It could thus play a significant role in shaping perceptions and approaches to issues of religious diversity.

Findings from the questionnaire survey

There were clear differences in the extent to which organisations from different religious traditions said their members experienced unfair treatment in education. For nearly every aspect of education covered in the questionnaire, a higher proportion of respondents from Muslim, Sikh and Hindu organisations reported unfair treatment than was the case for Christian, Jewish, Buddhist or Bahá'í organisations.

In addition, whilst a large majority of the Christian and Jewish organisations who reported unfair treatment said it was occasional, a relatively high proportion of Muslim organisations, in particular, said it was frequent.

Education was also a particular area of concern for NRM/Pagan respondents. However, it was the case for most faith groups that aspects of the education system were second only to the media, and roughly on a par with employment, in the extent to which unfair treatment was indicated by organisations from within that tradition

Schools

- Unfair treatment in schools was reported by more organisations, and was said to be more frequent, than unfair treatment in higher education or by education authorities.
- The behaviour of school pupils was a concern for nearly all traditions: it was indicated as a frequent or occasional problem by more than three quarters of respondents from Jewish, Hindu, Muslim and Sikh organisations and 60 per cent of Christian respondents.
- A similarly high proportion of respondents from Muslim and Sikh organisations, 14 out of 18 NRM/Pagan organisations and 10 out of 11 black-led Christian organisations said their members experienced frequent or occasional unfair treatment from school teachers – something that was reported by under 40 per cent of other Christian or Jewish organisations.

Other aspects of schooling that drew numerous claims of unfair treatment from some religious traditions were the RE curriculum and/or the teaching of RE. Most Muslim, Hindu, Sikh, NRM and Pagan organisations said their members experienced unfair treatment in these areas, with many saying the problem was frequent rather than occasional. By contrast, there were relatively few complaints about Citizenship Studies from any tradition, although in this context it should be noted that this curriculum area is not yet well known.

Arrangements for collective worship in schools were perceived as at least occasionally unfair by the majority of organisations from nearly all religions other than Christianity. Unfair treatment arising from the policies and practices of schools were reported by around two thirds or more of Muslim and Sikh organisations, compared with under 30 per cent of Christian organisations.

Specific examples of unfair treatment in schools that were given by respondents included the following:

- admissions (Hindus, Muslims)
- curriculum (inter-faith, Muslims, Sikhs, Zoroastrians)
- dress (Hindus, Muslims, Sikhs)
- funding (Sikhs, Zoroastrians)
- holidays (Jews, Muslims)
- marginalisation (Jains, Muslims, Zoroastrians)
- timetables (Jews, Muslims)

Unfair treatment in schools: quotes from the postal survey

Buddhists: *"no recognition of Buddhism", "Buddhism not taught", "emphasis on Christian teaching", "Buddhism badly taught and misunderstood", "children not accepted from Buddhist primary school", "name calling"*

Hindus: *"teachers' unfair attention to Asians", "told not to wear the Kunti-Mala", "selection of Asians in Roman Catholic school", "token treatment of Hindus", "name calling", "racial and physical abuse"*

Inter-faith: *"traditional bias", "RE Syllabus unfair", "misunderstood and excluded from the curriculum", "lack of awareness", "name calling"*

Jains: *"provision of special diets"*

Jews: *"examinations on religious holidays", "teachers stress Jews killed Jesus", "coverage of orthodox Jews", "verbal abuse", "right wing groups in schools"*

Muslims: *"sex education and dress", "provision of halal food", "no Islamic teacher", "dress, worship and exams", "child attacked because of faith", "no festival holiday", "a boy told to shave his head", "prevented from class due to dress", "understanding of cultural diversity", "teacher used insulting language", "lack of consideration for customs", "have to participate in mixed swimming", "prayer facilities"*

NRMs/Pagans: *"schools fail to cover Paganism", "lack of inclusion in RE", "Halloween banned by LEA", "refusal to include Paganism in curriculum", "curriculum is Christian biased", "spiritualism has no space in curriculum", "pupil forced to leave school", "ridicule", "bullying"*

Sikhs: *"teaching of Punjabi not being encouraged", "not allowed to wear Five Ks", "students taunted for wearing Turban", "abuse by peers because of name", "Sikhs excluded from policy making", "harassment by white students"*

Zoroastrians: *"Zoroastrians completely marginalised", "funding for religious schools"*

Higher education

- Around two thirds or more of Muslim organisations reported unfair treatment from the behaviour of staff and students in higher education, and from the policies and practices of universities/colleges.
- Students were also mentioned by two thirds or more of Jewish and Sikh organisations, and by 5 of the 7 black-led churches answering this question.
- Whilst over 40 per cent of Christian organisations mentioned the behaviour of staff and students, only around half this proportion said their members had experienced unfair treatment from the policies and practices of universities or colleges.

Unfair treatment at universities/colleges: quotes from the postal survey

Jews: *"student union politics", "events scheduled on religious days", "exams set on religious days", "right wing groups"*

Muslims: *"core texts had anti-Islamic strains", "hard to obtain prayer rooms"*

NRMs/Pagans: *"Pagan Society blocked", "patronising attitude that British equals Christian"*

Sikhs: *"admissions to university"*

Education authorities

A majority of Muslim, Sikh, black-led Christian and NRM organisations said their members experienced frequent or occasional unfair treatment from education officials, or the policies and practices of education authorities. The equivalent proportion for other Christian traditions was under a quarter.

The specific examples of unfair treatment covered similar ground to the examples given above for schools.

Local interviews

Interviews and meetings were conducted across the four fieldwork locations and with a range of national organisations. They included education specialists, local authority education staff, and individuals from among a range of religious communities with experience of education as either staff or students.

Attitudes of school teachers

A significant number of interviewees referred to particular difficulties still encountered by Hindu, Muslim and Sikh children after decades with a substantial presence in the education system. It was reported that some teachers are very negative towards, and apparently sometimes also seek actively to undermine, the religious beliefs and practices of Muslim pupils and parents. Furthermore, this was seen as being often done *"under the guise of equal opportunities"*, or because they think that Muslim beliefs and practices are *"fundamentalist"* or *"silly"*. Examples given included encouraging Muslim girls to meet boys and arguing against arranged marriages, as well as arranging mixed outings without consultation with parents or regard for their feelings and concerns. Pigs feature commonly in early-age books and activities, and teachers were reported as trying to push the pupils into saying the word "pig" when this can be felt to be polluting. One Hindu educationalist recalled Sikh children being embarrassed by teachers who derided them and their hair by saying things like *"why can't they chop off that bun?"*

It was noted that because of the status and power of teachers, their negative attitudes and behaviour can then have an adverse influence on the behaviour of other students. A Jehovah's Witness explained that:

> If a teacher gives a student a hard time in the class, then you can guarantee that the other students will do so at lunchtime. The reality is that a six-year-old is not intellectually able to articulate his or her views when challenged by teachers.

However, even for parents there can be difficulties in explaining to staff the importance to them and their children of the school trying to accommodate their family beliefs and practices:

> Every time a child starts a new school, the parents have to go in and make a stand. The problem is that there are a lot of grey areas, and what might be an issue or okay with some parents won't be for others. You end up having to explain to teachers, and not all parents say the same thing. The outcome of these sorts of encounters depends on the particular person's level of articulateness. I know this isn't intended as a form of persecution, but it involves starting from a negative view of the issue at hand.

With particular reference to the identity of Muslim children in schools, a white, female, educational development specialist pointed out that:

Any request to do even a small thing like make cards for Ramadan or have a party is seen as having to bend over backwards. They state that Ramadan makes children tired, and while Christmas often makes them overly excited and inattentive, they still work around this. There is no willingness to work around the results of fasting.

Ignorance of the religions of interviewees was particularly marked with regard to members of the smaller religious groups that are often seen as less 'mainstream'. One parent reported that when a teacher was going around the room asking children what faith they belonged to and his son said he was a Bahá'í, the teacher exclaimed that he had never heard of this religion and that he thought that the boy was making it up. Similarly, a member of the Jehovah's Witnesses recounted that when his son corrected a Religious Education teacher who said that Jehovah's Witnesses don't believe in Christ, the teacher argued with him. As one Jehovah's Witness interviewee concluded, there were particular and marked problems experienced by smaller religious groups that are often perceived as being less 'mainstream', but that even pupils within Christianity can have difficulties within the education system, since:

Anyone with a strong identity as a faith, even within Christianity, has trouble.

Facilities and dress
A group of mainly Muslim Asian school students identified the following problems:

Mixed showers
Despite pleas for curtains in the changing rooms, it took years to get these. The students found that the school had great difficulty in seeing how their needs were very similar to other students' concerns about modesty or discomfort. One youth worker noted that, in his school, he supported the same issue for white students who were over-weight and who also wanted curtains for greater privacy. Similar problems and issues exist with regard to mixed swimming.

Clothing
One woman noted that although it is now much more common to see girls wearing headscarves at school, when she was younger they were not allowed to do this because they violated the uniform code. As a result, they would take them off when they got to school and put them back on again afterwards. Similarly, these young people found it hard to understand why school staff and administrators asserted that they could not play sports appropriately or effectively whilst wearing leggings.

Arts activities

Others raised the problem of drawing, especially for Muslim and Bahá'í pupils. This can raise difficulties due to the injunctions of their religious traditions concerning visual representation of living forms. A white, female, education development specialist reported that such students often do not take home the pictures they draw in school and that they often have to be creative in order to avoid violating religious tenets. For example, one Bahá'í parent recalled her daughter being required to draw a picture of the burning bush when dealing with the story of Moses from the Hebrew scriptures. Upon asking her mother if that was allowed (which it was not), she managed to get around it by drawing flames and saying the bush was inside the flames.

Collective worship

A white, Welsh, education officer who is personally a Jehovah's Witness noted that, with respect to the current requirements for collective worship and assemblies, there were particularly acute problems for those parents wanting to exercise their legal right for their children to "*opt out*". He felt that current practice tends to highlight pupils' differences and to disrupt the process of community-building that it might be intended to support. Having permission to opt out of collective worship is not the same as having one's religion recognised or validated. It may also have other negative effects. The education officer recalled his own experience as an illustration of how children who opt out of collective worship are often made to feel:

> *When I was a child, the school assembly was in the Great Hall, with the youngest sitting up front. Every day, I had to come into the hall after worship with all those who were late, although I had formally opted out of assembly. It always drew extra attention, and was embarrassing. I think I might even have been seen as a problem child because I was always coming in late and not participating.*

The education officer highlighted the paradoxes involved. He explained that schools often do poorly in inspections of their provision for collective worship and assemblies. The format of these occasions has frequently been changed to accommodate the growing diversity of the school population so that they no longer follow traditional patterns. However, parents do still withdraw children and, when they do so, they are concerned about their children missing out on group time. A male, African-Caribbean, youth worker remarked that what he perceived as a current bias towards Christian education and assembly "*is evidence of the government going backwards*".

Religious education

Parents and young people frequently cited examples of the ways in which schools and teachers failed to include, recognise or reflect their religious identities and beliefs. This was especially the case with respect to the treatment, in religious education, of the smaller religious minorities, since model syllabi do not give much visibility to these groups. Such lack of recognition said to affect children's self-esteem. A parent from the Church of Jesus Christ of Latter-day Saints explained:

> They were doing the major religions and my son wanted to tell the kids in his class and assembly about the Church, and was upset about not being able to. He was later allowed to explain it to his class but not in the school assembly – because it was at the discretion of his class teacher who allowed him because he was presenting to his friends in the class, as opposed to the assembly, where, in that context, it was said that Latter-day Saints was not a Christian topic...

One young Zoroastrian girl described her efforts to tell fellow students and teachers that it was her New Year's day and that she "*just wanted someone to know*". But she reported that, in religious education, they only cover what are seen as the 'main' religions and that "*being a 'minority' religion makes us feel less important*".

On the other hand, where schools have made efforts to respond to religious diversity, Christians can sometimes feel that their religion is being pushed aside or trivialised by comparison with the coverage of other religions:

> There almost seems to be an embarrassment about doing Christian things. We have to apologise for being Christian. We have our children doing all manner of exotic dances and eating foods, but...It's sad Christian children are not taught about their own religions; that Christianity is overridden by other faiths. We should have a say. Years ago there were not as many faiths. Now we're overrun. Things have changed.

Several Christians added:

> When Diwali takes place and other such holidays, you get the full content in RE; it's celebrated in assemblies, rigorously done. When it comes to Easter, you get bunny rabbits and daffodils. At Christmas you get snowmen.

The group of school students referred to earlier felt that Christian teachers should teach Islam and Muslim teachers teach Christianity, so that teachers from each religion would have to take on board material about another religion. A male, Asian, youth advisor noted that: "*it is important that young people get used to seeing this mix*".

Attendance

Religious holidays can sometimes conflict with mandatory or key educational events. Parents and students are then put into the position of having to choose between their religion and important school-based events. One Hindu recalled that a University's graduation ceremony had been held on the first day of Diwali, and that an inoculation day at school was scheduled on the Hindu New Year. A Jewish interviewee noted that the start of a postgraduate programme of university study coincided with the Jewish high holy day of Yom Kippur. These interviewees drew attention to the problem of having, in such circumstances, to make hard choices. They felt that, at least in terms of major holidays, things could be made easier either by more informed scheduling or by allowing more flexibility in relation to time off for religious festivals. As one interviewee observed:

> *I don't understand. These are education institutions. The holidays are even printed on calendars now.*

One Muslim woman, illustrating the problem of being given time off as "*a favour*" rather than as an established holiday, reported that Eid recently fell on a Saturday, so the school didn't "*bother*" to provide any school days off.

Islamic schools

A number of interviewees raised the issue of separate education for Muslim children. One group felt that, in general, Islamic schools could offer a conducive and appropriate environment and that, specifically, they could avoid conflicts around issues such as sex education. One informant expressed the conviction that:

> *...religious organisations can run schools better because they are independent and are supported by the community they serve.*

A white, female, educational specialist noted that it is also important to consider the point that such schools allow the students to attend school without the constant fear of the effects of racism, bullying, and harassment.

In contrast to this, others, both from within religious traditions and communities and outside them, expressed a concern that separate schools *"don't create harmonious society"*, and that they may even create further divisions. One Christian educationalist acknowledged that, as compared with the many Church of England, Catholic and Jewish schools, the difficulty of getting state funding for Islamic schools *"is an historical unfairness"*. However, he also stated that:

> *Just because there is one not particularly helpful way of schooling that we have to live with, we shouldn't extenuate division by using an unhelpful model.*

With regard to the variety of forms of education within the Muslim community, interviewees drew attention to reports of mullahs caning children, insisting that: *"it's not okay just because it happened in the mosque"*. However, an education specialist noted that in these debates there is a tendency to focus on extremes. She noted that there are never reports of how much Muslim children might like going to mosque schools or the extent to which such activities may contribute to the schools' objectives in terms of developing extra-curricular interests and activities. Others observed that many people are very quick to assume that Islamic schools will not uphold national curriculum requirements or recruit qualified teachers.

Finding solutions

Respondents to the postal survey were asked to suggest ways in which unfair treatment in education could be tackled. The three main suggestions were:

- public education programmes/greater awareness
- policy reviews to promote equal treatment
- better training.

Other suggestions included more teaching of comparative religion, greater consultation between school governors and religious groups, voluntary codes of practice, and changes in the law or the introduction of new law.

Views expressed in the local interviews are set out below.

Service provision and policy

In some cases, schools have taken innovative steps towards meeting the needs of children and parents of various religions by establishing active relationships with local religious communities and organisations. In one of the local research areas, several schools had endeavoured to meet the needs of the Muslim population. One of these schools, for example, has separate assemblies and had invited a local imam to be involved in contributing to student welfare. One Asian, male, policy worker felt that such steps represent a good way forward:

> ...as long as everyone knows what they're working toward and stays on track...It's important for the future to create links between the many different types of educational contexts and experiences that many students have. Some may go to maintained schools, then to madrassas in the afternoon, and possibly homework centres in the evening – they have completely different experiences in each context and that it would be a powerful thing to get all the sectors working together...

Another white, Welsh, male educationalist reported that, in one school, Jehovah's Witness pupils, overseen by a volunteer, are allowed to structure their own study group in lieu of collective worship and that this works very well, even though it might not be fully in line with the established rules.

A number of interviewees underlined that it was important for parents to take active steps to help positive change. One Bahá'í parent, for example, had provided the local school with a "pastoral care" booklet so that teachers and administrators could be made aware of pertinent issues and requirements for Bahá'í children.

Role models

One Hindu former teacher stated that, in order to bring about change, there is a need for key role models among both teachers and students. She recalled that she was determined to be counted on her own merits and wanted to prove that she could excel, in spite of the stereotyped expectations she experienced due to her traditional dress. She organised a Diwali play that, in due course, became well known, well funded and an acknowledged model for others. She also designed physical education lessons to show that trouser suits did not impede proper physical exercise.

One young person noted that much had changed in his school over the past five years. But he underlined that this had come about due to the willingness of himself and others to speak out. He said that they had been able to teach their teachers first and then the other students. Yet despite this progress:

> ...whenever you have a particular need or whatever, it's seen as a major problem. Even when you do something really good, you're still made to feel negative about it; like it's also a problem.

Others also noted that they had to "fight for" or "make an issue of everything", that "you have to take it rather than being given it", and that there is "a lot of begrudging". A teacher and youth worker commented that this can, in itself, lead to further difficulties for the individuals involved since:

> ...when you do work hard at things or are trying to institute the changes you see are needed and are not supported by the administration, so you have to do it all on your own, you're seen as promoting yourself, empire building, or promotion seeking.

Holidays

A white, male, education officer, in an area where some recognition had been given to holidays associated with minority religious traditions, said he wished they had not made such a change. This was because he felt that the Muslim festival of Eid, especially, "creates an administrative nightmare" since the exact day is not known in advance. A Jehovah's Witness parent noted that it is important to have recognised holidays, but also that schools "do need 190 school days, and staff say they can't deliver in the time given; you have to sympathise with teachers on this point". He also recognised that if pupils opt out of some activities, the teachers have to provide alternatives and that "teachers have a lot on their plates".

Expansion of Religious Education

A number of interviewees from within religious communities and traditions argued for both more, and better-rounded, religious education. Some argued strongly that RE needed to be seen as something more than an aspect of cultural education. Approaching religions in terms of their own "theological" self-understandings might lead to better understanding and relationship-building among young people. This would also help in addressing the religious diversity of white indigenous society, too. For example:

Mormon children should be able to educate others about what the Latter-day Saints church is about as is done with Asian people. They are not ethnic/cultural minorities, but a religious minority, and then not seen as Christian and thus unaccepted. RE and the curriculum as a whole focuses on ethnic issues, forgetting the diversity of the white indigenous society.

Collective worship

A range of interviewees noted that the Education Act provision for collective worship was often circumvented by schools. A number argued that collective worship/assemblies needed to be abolished either altogether, or at least in the form in which they are currently framed in law. It was felt that removing what was widely perceived as a Christian bias would give more space to achieving objectives such as the promotion of tolerance and harmony in all-school assemblies. It was also felt that it would contribute to the development of Religious Education as a curriculum subject in its own right, rather than something to be confused with education in a particular religious tradition.

The National Curriculum

There was a plea for flexibility and alternative provision for students who need to opt out of activities such as music, dance and swimming that can be in tension, or even in conflict, with religious beliefs. It was argued that diversity *"should be a cross-cutting theme"* in curricula, and that this should especially be the case in rural schools and other areas where diversity was either not so great or so apparent. It was pointed out that diversity issues pertain to wider national contexts, not just those of the school community and its immediate locality, and that this should be better addressed in inspections. The provision of culturally sensitive materials and support was advocated.

Citizenship education

There were also pleas for a greater focus on citizenship education and for this to debate how our diverse society should work; how this has come about; what equal opportunities mean and how they work. Others recommended expanding a citizenship-based curriculum in order to 'mainstream' the ethos of diversity and anti-discrimination into the goal of national identity-building. They argued that *"if you want to change society you have to begin with the children"*. Hopes were expressed that if this was done, then there might be a possibility of moving beyond the generations in which racism has flourished, whilst forming and involving new generations of interrelationships in building a common culture.

Monitoring

It was often argued that diversity of all kinds should be more 'mainstreamed'. A white, male, local authority staff member noted that because there are so many current initiatives related to the report of the Stephen Lawrence Inquiry and to projects of the Commission for Racial Equality, his organisation was trying to get an equalities officer post established in order to work with individual schools on developing their policies. He felt that schools needed to monitor student intakes more accurately in order better to understand and serve pupils' needs. He reported that schools that have larger minority populations are often better linked into the local communities and are aware of such needs. By contrast, in the case of schools with predominantly white populations, religious minorities may be either more assimilated or more reticent. In particular, he felt that such schools require a better understanding of differences between religion and ethnicity, which were felt to be too often confused with one another.

Employment

A Muslim woman knew at the end of an interview that she would not get the job because, unlike the other candidates, she did not shake the interviewer's hand. When she declined, he jolted back....He wants to hire someone he can relate to.
It's very subtle.
An interviewee

For those in work and those seeking to gain access to it, employment is an area of central significance to their individual lives and to those of their families, relating closely to personal esteem as well as economic opportunity. For the wider society, employment provides a means by which the skills, talents, and enterprise of individuals can contribute towards the creation of financial and cultural wealth. It is therefore an area in which it is very important that individuals and groups are not denied fair opportunities on grounds that are unrelated to their ability to do the job.

Findings from the questionnaire survey

- For organisations from most religious traditions, employment was one of the three areas of life (along with education and the media) where their members were most likely to experience unfair treatment.
- The majority of Muslim, Sikh, and Hindu organisations reported unfair treatment in almost every aspect of employment covered in the questionnaire, and most of the NRM/Pagan organisations indicated likewise. Muslim organisations were more likely than Sikh or Hindu organisations to indicate that this unfair treatment was 'frequent' rather than 'occasional'.
- In almost all traditions, fewer organisations reported unfair treatment in the voluntary sector than in the private or public sectors.
- Two or three times as many Christian organisations reported unfairness in the behaviour of managers and colleagues as reported unfairness in the policies and practices of employers. This distinction was much less marked for the other faith groups, who were more likely to detect unfairness in policy and practice as well as in behaviour.
- The small number of black-led groups responding to these questions were more likely to report unfair treatment than other Christian organisations.

The private sector

Around three quarters or more of the Sikh, Muslim and Hindu organisations said their members experienced unfair treatment from private sector managers or colleagues. This compares with just over 40 per cent of the Christian organisations, and lower proportions in some of the other religions (eg Buddhists and Bahá'ís). Moreover, whilst 25 out of 55 Muslim organisations said unfair treatment by private sector managers was 'frequent', this was the case for only 5 per cent of the Christian organisations.

The proportion of Christian organisations saying their members experienced unfairness from the policies and practices of private sector employers dropped to around a quarter. This compares, for example, with 27 out 31 Sikh organisations reporting unfairness in private sector employment policies. It was Muslims again, however, who were the most likely to say that unfairness was frequent.

The public sector

Some religious traditions reported marginally less unfair treatment in the public sector than the private sector, but the differences were not large. A higher proportion of Muslim organisations continued to report 'frequent' unfair treatment than was the case for other traditions.

Organisations from some religions (eg Muslim, Sikh, Christian) reported slightly more unfairness in public sector employment practices than in policies.

The voluntary sector

Fewer organisations indicated unfairness from either individuals or employers in voluntary sector. In addition, Muslim organisations were much more likely to indicate that unfairness in this sector was occasional than was the case with public and private sector employers.

Jobcentres and employment agencies

Respondents were again asked about the attitudes and behaviour of staff, and the policies and practices of the organisations. Muslim organisations were generally the most likely to state that their members experienced unfair treatment from these agencies, and were again more likely than other traditions to indicate that unfairness was frequent. All traditions, however, reported less unfairness by jobcentres and employment agencies than by private and public sector employers.

Examples

Specific examples of unfair treatment in employment that were given by respondents included the following:

- Dress restrictions (Muslims, Sikhs, inter-faith)
- Working on religious days/holidays (Christians, Jains, Jews, NRMs, Pagans, Sikhs)
- Lack of respect and ignorance of religious customs (Hindus, Jews, Muslims, Zoroastrians)
- Application and recruitment practices (Christians, Muslims, NRMs, Sikhs, Zoroastrians, inter-faith)
- Promotion prospects (Sikhs).

Unfair treatment in employment: quotes from the postal survey

Christians: *"being refused work"*, *"working on Sundays/Good Friday"*, *"asked to lie for company"*, *"ethical standards compromised"*, *"verbal abuse"*, *"sexual material put in locker"*, *"bullying"*, *"profanity"*, *"exclusion from associations"*, *"disrespect"* – *"God squad"*, *"ridicule"*, *"anti-Catholicism"*

Hindus: *"indirect racism"*, *"white supremacy in good jobs"* *"low job survival rate"*, *"low representation in civil service"*

Inter-faith: *"preconception of abilities"*, *"colleagues' jokes about hijab"*, *"verbal abuse"*

Jains: *"holidays coincide with work"*

Muslims: *"woman lost job for wearing a hijab"*, *"Islamophobia"*, *"prayer facilities"* *"refused employment because of dress code"*, *"stereotyping"*, *"low representation"*

NRM/Pagans: *"can't admit beliefs"*, *"enforced Christian holidays"*, *"harassed by manager"*, *"refusing to take recruitment ads"*

Sikhs: *"excuses made for rejections"*, *"wearing of 5k's"*, *"promotion for whites only"*, *"discriminate beard/turban"*

Local interviews

Interviews and meetings were conducted across the four local areas and with a range of relevant national organisations. These included human resources and equalities officers in public institutions; representatives of business development organisations; and individual employees from religious communities/groups.

Applying for jobs

Interviewees stated that wearing traditional or religious dress to interviews was a source of great concern. An advice worker recalled being asked during an interview, *"would you be wearing that?"* (in other words, her head scarf) and noted that the woman interviewer would not even say the word. Another woman decided not to apply for a job that required submitting the job application in person rather than posting it, because she felt she would automatically be judged negatively by her visual appearance. She acknowledged that this assumption might be wrong, but that she just couldn't face having to wonder what aspect of an array of possibilities might keep her from getting the job.

As well as appearance, social norms related to cultural and religious traditions can also lead to unfair treatment:

> *A Muslim woman knew at the end of an interview that she would not get the job because, unlike the other candidates, she did not shake the interviewer's hand. When she declined, he jolted back. You see, he becomes prevented from engaging in the same social practices he's used to. He wants to hire someone he can relate to. It's very subtle.*

Offensive behaviour at work

At a school, an employee was cajoled by the head teacher into trying to participate in a "crocodile dance", with the head teacher saying *"shake those hips"*. She felt that the intention of this was purposely to make her feel as uncomfortable as possible.

A Muslim woman working in a voluntary organisation reported that a fellow employee who had behaved negatively towards her was able to give her a final *"kick in the teeth"* on the occasion of his leaving lunch. For this meal, in an office kitchen with no ventilation, he cooked bacon butties. This had the literal effect of smoking her out, whilst he declared to the group, *"there's nothing like a bacon butty to bring everyone together"*. She said it was the most offensive thing she had experienced in her life. Given that the person worked in the voluntary sector, she felt it was even more shocking.

A number of other interviewees drew attention to similar conflicts between their religious beliefs and social activities related to work. One woman said of these activities, such as leaving parties, that:

> ... you're seen to be anti-social [if you don't drink, etc.], especially because social norms are inherently exclusionary.

Yet she also noted that some of this is changing, and that people now "act less weird" if she drinks fruit juice rather than alcohol.

Dress codes

A Sikh woman, who worked in a medium sized bakery, related the following story through her son:

> For 8 years, it was never a problem. Then, for one and a half years they picked on this (Sikh) woman for wearing her bangle. Finally, they moved her to a different part of the [organisation]. They said she must take it off, but she said no. Representatives from the Sikh temple had a meeting with Personnel to explain, but they said no because it was classed as jewellery.

Other interviewees mentioned that tests were done to see if there were any bacteria in the bangle, and that these came out negative. They also made the point that her apron sleeves covered the bangle. This controversy had important knock-on effects for other Sikh women who came forward in support of this woman to state that they themselves also wore bangles, and who then also became subject to harassment by other employees as well as by the management. The woman lost her case at a tribunal, but after years of fighting a special sleeve was developed, and the management and staff were required to attend diversity training.

Others who commented on this case believed that it represented clear cut discrimination, especially as a very persuasive and clear argument was made by religious community representatives, and other employees were wearing wedding rings. However, a white, male, employment tribunal representative (and who was not associated with the case) commented:

...knowing how diverse society is, sometimes situations are just unfair. People will have to be aware of say, hygiene regulations, and if they have to wear a bangle, they may have to do something else either within the organisation or as a job. You have to find a balance...the average employer couldn't really care less about religion unless it affects the running of her or his business which usually can be covered by race protections.

An education professional recounted a case of a colleague in which a formal charge of racism was not upheld after an internal investigation. In this case:

The head teacher asked the staff member why she was wearing a hijab, and if she was "forced" to wear it. She also brought up health and safety requirements and asked, in terms of hygiene, if she would wash her scarf everyday...The head teacher convinced the LEA that she had such conversations like that all the time with all her staff....

Holidays and days off

Examples were given that illustrate what can happen when managers are approached about religious festivals. One employee recalled that a colleague who mentioned that a meeting scheduled on a Friday took place on the Muslim festival of Eid was told "so what?".

A Christian interviewee remarked that:

There is now more sensitivity to not making people work [on Sundays]. Yet because of shift work, there is always a portion of the congregation that is always missing because some feel the need to support other staff, or due to the threat of losing their job or promotion.

Self censorship

Two Pagans reported that they feel that they have to take measures to keep their religious lives secret while at work. One said that, if confronted about his Pagan identity, he would need to lie. As a consequence, however, they fear they may be perceived as being suspect and dishonest and they were worried that negative stereotypes would be perpetuated if anyone found out.

Interviewees said it was often assumed that people from religious traditions with a reputation for seeking converts (eg Evangelical Christians, Unificationists and Bahá'ís) were engaged in mission activity at work even when they were just talking casually about themselves.

Communicating needs

The work environment can make it difficult for staff to communicate their needs. One young woman reported that while she personally has had a positive response to discussions and requests, her friends in other professions and industries have had significant difficulties, especially over matters of dress.

> Their employers don't want their employees to wear traditional forms of dress and aren't interested in knowing about them. It's troubling that they don't really have any recourse other than leaving their jobs – although they have not been sacked over the dress issue, they have not been accepted. But I'm not sure if they have approached their employers and have been able to explain properly – they might be too frightened or worried about fitting in.

She went on to explain that:

> ... it is hard for an employee, and a young person, to broach this subject; you don't want to be seen making demands after being hired. I often feel somewhat uncomfortable and shy in this situation...It is much better and easier to address if an employer meets you half way – by asking.

Finding solutions

Organisations responding to the postal survey were asked to suggest ways in which unfair treatment in employment could be tackled. The three main suggestions were:

- public education programmes/school education
- policy reviews to promote equal treatment
- greater flexibility in employment and acceptance of religion

Other suggestions included a change in law; reviewing and regulating recruitment and promotion; and better consultation between employees and employer.

Accommodating religious diversity in the work place poses a number of dilemmas for employers. One interviewee pointed out that:

> ... there's an element of a "Pandora's box" whereby even though the staff should feel empowered, there is the fear that if you recognise the diversity of the staff, they will start asking for unmeetable demands.

Policy development and training

Even where employers wish to respond to diversity, they may lack effective knowledge of religious differences and where to go to find reliable information:

> Some people or organisations might not pursue it, because even if they find out information known about some religious communities, there are still so many others.

The importance to employers of community partnerships and of central sources of information about religious communities was often noted. Local networks of advisors are needed, but an advice worker noted that there is also a need for:

> ...some kind of advisory body on a more national or regional level, given peoples' lack of knowledge and lack of pursuing it, whether for fear of offending or that they don't think about things religiously, and because there are so many different communities and sources of information... Such a body or source of information regarding all religions could also be consulted by schools, universities, charities, and business.

Yet a policy officer noted that even when an employer does have access to knowledge and is aware of the importance of educating staff, "training can be seen as a punitive measure". As an example, one large public organisation had a diversity conference in which sessions were attended by 3,500 employees over two days:

> It was seen as very brave and very scary [for those putting on the event] ...Some people thought it was brilliant and were blown away by how good it was. They thought it was the best thing the [organisation] had done and were enthused it was prepared to deal with these issues. There was also the other end of the continuum, which, when asked what further training was needed, one comment noted "training for repatriating the black b******s". There were people who didn't want to be there, who wouldn't sit down, who talked through the whole session. One comment said that the person couldn't comment on the session because she or he couldn't hear it for all of the racist and sexist comments of the group sitting in front of him or her...

The inclusion of religion in official equalities statements has been an important development in a number of companies. However, a white, female, policy officer noted that "It is easy to say these things, but much harder to bring in change through policies". A number of other interviewees stressed that the formulation of policies do not, of itself, guarantee effective implementation. A white, female, policy officer of a small voluntary sector organisation noted that:

An equal opps statement doesn't tell you anything. It doesn't provide interpretive guidelines; it doesn't guarantee a commitment. There are so many issues – it's a minefield.

There can be difficulties for organisations as they try to respond to the multiple challenges of diversity in a measured and realistic way. A white, female, staff member of a political authority explained that:

We're just now working through policies addressing women and race – we have to try to get those right and then expand.

Even though equal opportunities policies may be problematic an Asian, male, council employee nevertheless felt that:

...having religion included in the equal opportunities policy makes a lot [of positive initiatives] possible and contributes to a positive atmosphere. If you didn't include religion from the outset, you wouldn't be recognising what may be an integral side of an individual...

A representative of a national employer pointed out that, in their organisation, robust equal opportunities policies actually saved money and that effective equal opportunity policies served to ensure a better working environment, better efficiency and less absenteeism.

Another advice worker noted that, whilst the education of employers is important, and that staff development also has a role to play:

... what is missing are practical steps, plans of actions and guidance for taking those steps; establishing a way of accommodating the differences and needs they are coming to understand......You need to make people aware, to have access to information, but you also need a way of making such things not optional, but obligations – establishing these as responsibilities is key; that's possibly where law comes in....but once you establish an obligation, you need to establish a way of following up by providing resources and guidance...

Small organisations

Although small organisations have particular challenges in accommodating diversity, a white, male, business development executive observed that they also have some advantages:

...chemistry is the most important factor in employee hiring and relations; they depend on it, not how politically correct a decision is. No matter how "pc" it is, it won't work. In smaller businesses, you sit down and have the same cup of tea with each other, talk about things. In this context, an employee might say to the employer, "Eid is coming up..." – that there might be some problems in that you don't know what day it will happen on, but it's discussed/known, and thus can be accommodated.

One professional observed that for small employers, little things can mean a lot, such as:

...a notice board, a table in the corner of the workplace where employees can have things that reflect who they are.

She believed that what is required is:

...a mandate that you have to acknowledge – even if it involves only one person – and a little flexibility. It doesn't require much in terms of money, space, or effort. Wouldn't small employers want to say they have a global workforce?

Scheduling to accommodate religious festivals and holy days can pose significant challenges for small employers. A white, male, business adviser pointed out that:

...the impact of one person can't be absorbed in the same way – support by enough staff to cover if time off is needed. Larger staffs have the benefit of having more diverse views, to balance out particular issues or needs.

However, it was also noted by a number of interviewees that employees can do a lot in terms of flexible support for each other. For example, in respect of a medium-sized advice unit linked with the local authority, an employee explained that:

In my organisation, Christian employees are supported on Christian holidays and vice versa. If there are two people wanting Boxing Day off, the priority goes to the Christian.

This works similarly for fasting during the Muslim month of Ramadan, where:

...non-Muslim employees hold down the fort during that time, and Muslim employees have done so at other times.

Large organisations

One example of an attempt to make religious diversity part of a corporate vision was an initiative by a health organisation to integrate spiritual care for its clients with its employment policies. This not only includes recognising religious needs, but caring for the needs of those who are not identified with a religion. In cultivating a multi-faith environment staff have set up:

> ...various partnerships with key religious organisations both local and outside the area – which have also flowed, in large part, from the people on the staff who are devout members, and working with them to build bridges with their communities, and training people to be bridges themselves.

At diversity training seminars representatives were provided from both the chaplaincy and from health quality assurance units. One staff member reported that working towards an increased level of service provision has "created a lot of good will – people moving forward together is priceless". He also explained that:

> ...spiritual care is also necessary for our staff...if they feel cared for they can better care for others...Staff with no religious beliefs have come to see me, and respect the role of chaplaincy/pastoral care, even if they don't agree with the particular doctrines.

In working with these dimensions he was convinced that:

> ...a robustly multi-faith approach provides a great deal of credibility.

Since this corporate vision was first established, steps were taken to develop an appropriate multi-faith chapel. However, with the potential Muslim user population reaching well over 50 per cent, one employee argued that the organisation still has a long way to go – for example, in the provision of proper washing facilities for Muslim prayers.

Another large education organisation had taken a different approach to the accommodation of religious diversity, striving to establish a "secular" policy and organisational environment, based on a philosophy of "acknowledge all, promote none". At the same time, as a contribution to implementing this, the organisation has created an inter-faith advisory committee in order to establish a stronger, two-way relationship with religious communities and leaders. A white, male, interviewee observed that the organisation's environment, whilst secular, does not promote secularism. It has sought to create a "neutral" space in which people can follow their own religions without one religion becoming predominant.

For example, rather than having a dedicated prayer room, a different room is allocated each day.

In this way the organisation sees all resources as being directed towards service provision, thus avoiding the possibility that one group might dominate the use of a single dedicated prayer room with this in itself becoming a source of tension. However, because they no longer *"deck the halls"* for Christmas, it was reported that there is some confusion among staff, who think that celebration is not allowed in any form, including the exchange of holiday cards:

> *As a secular college, we don't celebrate, but don't stop people from doing it.*

Other interviewees said the implementation of the "secular" policy was haphazard and inconsistent, and that this inconsistency destabilised both the staff and the client environment.

Legislation

A wide variety of views were expressed about the potential benefits or otherwise of law in tackling unfair treatment on the basis of religion in employment specifically. A white male, advice manager recalled that:

> *...with age discrimination, we had a voluntary code. All studies show it's not working. You'll always have good employers who have the foresight of the advantages of overcoming stereotypes, who have imagination.*

A white, female, policy manager felt that "the lack of mainstream religious equality is a national problem" and that equal opportunities policies at the local level can offer a more comprehensive approach than the currently quite narrow framework offered by the *Race Relations Act*:

> *It is probably time for the Race Relations Act be revised. It should include religion because it's so intertwined.*

A professional stated that the successful implementation of the Disability Discrimination Act had been hindered by the absence of enforcement measures. This same interviewee expressed the view that unfair treatment on the basis of religion could be addressed through legislation, but also that employers were in particular need of being able to see, and to draw upon, examples of good practice from elsewhere:

...you need to have champions who say "we're doing it!" along with good practice guidelines and demands from the top. You need reporting, bench-marking data, peer group pressure – it shouldn't require a lot of investment; often people are apt to say that they'd need too much money to do it...

One male, Asian, advice professional commented on the way in which legislation can serve to empower people to stand up for their own rights. For example, although the Sex Discrimination Act was thought to need further refinement:

...now you expect women to stand up. You don't need a policy to say what the policy should say. They are aware of their rights. An employer might not have a policy statement on maternity leave, but if an employee is pregnant, you go find out what their needs are, and what needs to happen....Having a bank of documents is not enough or necessary.

A white, female, business development specialist observed that:

You need worked examples for employers to draw on, especially if regulation is involved. Good practice examples are important, especially because they're more comprehensible – and are especially germane as they tell start up companies to emulate and evaluate the good practices of their competitors, which is a good way to pass it along as part of good business.

5   Criminal justice and immigration

....religious issues are creeping in. We have always taken race incidents as visible – because racism turns primarily on visible minorities. But things are becoming more subtle and more complicated.
(comment from a Police Inspector)

Criminal Justice

The Criminal Justice system does not directly impact upon the lives of all people. But whether as suspects, offenders or victims of crime, or as employees within the system, large numbers of people are directly or indirectly affected by it. Since the system embodies aspects of the power of the state, ordinary people who are caught up in it for one reason or another can feel especially vulnerable. Such vulnerability can be exacerbated by the experience of unfair treatment on the basis of religion.

Findings from the questionnaire survey

Many organisations did not have enough experience of the criminal justice system to be able to answer all the questions in this section of the questionnaire. Whilst questions about the police were answered by around 60-70 per of the organisations that returned questionnaires, and questions about lawyers and the courts by 50-60 per cent, the figures dropped to between 30 and 40 per cent for the questions on the prison and probation services.

The low number of responses from many religious traditions means that the findings in these areas can only be treated as very indicative. Overall, however, it was an area in which there were large gaps between the experiences of Muslim and Sikh organisations, on the one hand, and Christian organisations on the other. Responses from NRM/Pagan organisations suggested that unfair treatment was also common for this group.

Christian, Jewish, Buddhist and Bahá'í organisations were less likely to feel that their members experienced unfair treatment in the criminal justice system than in education or employment. For Muslim, Sikh and Hindu organisations, on the other hand, unfairness in the criminal justice system was about as likely as in these other areas.

Police

The questions about the police service revealed some sharp contrasts between religious groups. Buddhists, Bahá'ís, and most of the Christian traditions reported little or no unfair treatment, whereas two thirds or more of Muslim, Sikh and Hindu organisations reported unfairness both in the attitudes and behaviour of police officers, and in the practices of the police service. The handful of questionnaires from black-led Christian organisations and the responses from NRM/Pagan groups suggested that they experienced a similarly high level of unfair treatment. Over a third of Muslim organisations said that unfairness was 'frequent': a higher proportion than in the other traditions.

Organisations from most religious groups were more likely to indicate unfair treatment in the attitudes and behaviour of police officers than in the policies of the police service, with police practices falling somewhere between the two.

Unfair treatment from the police: quotes from the postal survey

Sikhs: *"racist police", "more suspicion and lack of understanding", "unequal treatment", "institutional racism in police", "arrested for wearing Kirpan", "police arrive late", "police undermine community"*

Muslims: *"police victimising Muslims", "dress stopping employment", "police delaying investigation", "stopped when in large groups", "spot checks", "made to feel uncomfortable", "police not doing anything", "stop searches by police"*

Hindus: *"police stop and search policy", "believe minorities cause crime", "stereotyping and prejudice", "no respect for older Asians", "police not responsive", "police don't give a priority"*

NRM/Pagans: *"police dawn raids", "institutional racism in the police", "ignorance of religion"*

Lawyers and the courts

The traditions that were most likely to report unfairness from the police service were also more likely to report unfairness from lawyers and the court service. Overall, however, fewer organisations in each tradition complained of unfair treatment from these sources, and when they did so, they were more likely to say it was 'occasional'.

Unfair treatment from the courts: quotes from the postal survey

Muslims: *"stereotyped regime", "in-built prejudice", "looked upon suspiciously"*

Sikhs: *"lack of respect for the holy book"*

NRMs/Pagans: *"only Christian oaths"*

Hindus: *"not providing the right advice"*

Prisons

Organisations were asked about the attitudes and behaviour of prison officers and inmates, as well as policy and practice in prisons. Allowing for the lower number of responses to this question, organisations from most religious traditions were more likely to report unfair treatment in prisons than from the police service. The variation between religions was still high: for example, 34 out of 38 Muslim organisations indicated unfair treatment from prison staff, compared with 21 out of 124 Christian organisations.

The attitudes and behaviour of prison officers was the aspect of prison life that was most likely to be picked out. In most traditions more organisations reported unfairness in prison practice than policy.

Unfair treatment in prisons: quotes from the postal survey

Buddhists: *"Buddhist chaplains under Christian control", "denied access to Buddhist chaplaincy", "obstruction by Anglican chaplains", "inadequate provision"*

Hindus: *"ignoring culture", "not provide right advice"*

Inter-faith: *"provision of holy book", "appropriate food"*

Jews: *"provision of kosher food", "individual hostility"*

Muslims: *"physical abuse", "lack of visiting", "Muslim chaplains work under Christian chaplains", "provision of halal food", "white favouritism"*

NRMs/Pagans: *"denied festival celebration", "intolerant prison chaplains", "no provision of Pagan Chaplains"*

Sikhs: *"lack knowledge in Sikh customs"*

The probation service

In most traditions those organisations who were able to answer questions on the probation service were less likely to indicate unfair treatment than was the case for all the other elements of the criminal justice system.

> *This was not so for Muslim organisations, however, with a higher proportion indicating unfair treatment from the probation service (around two in three) than from lawyers and the courts (around one in three).*

Unfair treatment in the probation service: quotes from the postal survey

Hindu: *"not provide right advice"*

Sikhs: *"not respect religious beliefs"*, *"asked to remove turbans"*,

Local interviews

The criminal justice system was not a major focus of the local interviews. Like the organisations responding to the postal survey, many people had limited experience in this area.

The police

Some of the most relevant interviews were with police representatives and centred upon police-community relations and multi-agency initiatives. Individuals and representatives of religious organisations also raised particular issues of concern, such as the need for more police coverage of places of worship, to which the response was often that there were insufficient resources.

Religion or race?

One woman who reported an incident as being religious harassment explained that the police could not seem to understand that it was a religious as distinct from a racist incident (she is white, her husband is from an ethnic minority, and their religious identity is not a visible one).

The problems involved in identifying the racist and/or religious dimensions of an incident were discussed with the police and with support workers. Many felt that a bully or perpetrator of harassment will ultimately use whatever vulnerabilities they attribute to their victim in order to inflict harm. An Asian female support worker described the difficulties that result:

Far be it for me to say that someone is not experiencing what they believe they are experiencing – for sometimes people don't realise what they are experiencing is racial harassment, or if, in describing their experience in terms of race, that what it actually is, is religious discrimination. People want the opportunity to sit down and explain what's going on...They should be given the opportunity to bring forward their experience and explain which one it is...

She also noted, however, that people will not come forward to report something unless they know there is an infrastructure to respond to and take up their concerns.

A police inspector noted that:

...an incident may start as a road rage incident and then move to racial insults, even if it wasn't initially motivated by race – there's the same problem with religion: it might begin as racial harassment but then elements of religion are brought into it.

One Police Constable said that by hiring Asian staff (in particular, Asian women staff to liase with Asian women) his department had seen an increase in reporting and programme development in that area of work. A Police Inspector noted that monitoring of issues in relation to religion is important since:

...religious issues are creeping in. We have always taken race incidents as visible – because racism turns primarily on visible minorities. But things are becoming more subtle and more complicated.

There were varying opinions on the importance and practicality of adding religion to police incident monitoring forms. At present, anti-Semitism might be the only religious-related information -recorded in such reports. Concerns were expressed about whether including religious identity as a part of crime reports would be negatively or suspiciously received by victims of crime. A Police Constable noted, however, that monitoring religion ultimately would not affect the way cases are handled, and should not affect the level of investigation:

...it's all about the satisfaction of the victim, rather than treating all victims the same, you have to adapt the investigation to the victim.

Another PC felt that any information that will tell him more about the case and those involved was important, "*You must know, so you have to ask to find out*".

Community consultation and involvement

In response to issues arising from diversities, one local police service had put a lot of effort into developing community networks. It has a religious representative on its advisory board and also hosts a multi-cultural evening, inviting close to 500 people to attend. As a consequence, two-way communication is easier. A Police Constable noted the importance of having an advisory group, and/or a network of people:

> ...who can give good advice as opposed to representing a particular community...If there's an incident, we invite them in on the case as early as possible to monitor and advise on investigation; these networks are also important for feeding back good news and positive results into the communities.

An Asian female advice worker recalled that when a series of bombs recently went off in her locality, the police very helpfully and proactively called a meeting, recognising that minorities were feeling very insecure. However, a white, female, specialist in diversity training reported that a similar gesture in a different location yielded a situation in which the police called ethnic minority contacts to attend a meeting, but completely forgot the Jewish community and therefore did not seem to be paying attention to issues relating to anti-semitism.

Accommodating religious needs

One constable noted that, ultimately, providing prayer facilities for detainees who are Muslims is straightforward, *"you only need a mat and a compass"*. He also felt that doing this was in the interests of the police service in order to avoid situations in which the suspect felt unduly pressured or distracted because he or she needs to fulfil religious requirements during the time of the interview. More generally, the officer also added that it is necessary to encourage religious groups to inform officers about their needs.

Training

A number of examples were given of police training. These mainly focused on conveying information about appropriate behaviour in the context of standard police work. This included the removal of shoes in places of worship; being accompanied by a female officer (or waiting for one to arrive) before questioning women in some communities; rules for going into mosques and for handling the Qur'an; and the need to avoid speaking of the Prophet in offensive ways. Officers were said to be not necessarily sure what do or what to ask. Therefore training, and the ability to build effective relationships with diverse communities were seen as key measures.

The prison service

The local interviews did not give rise to much exploration of issues related to the prison service. However, a member of the Roman Catholic clergy reported that Roman Catholics are experiencing increasing difficulties in a nearby prison. He observed that:

> ...you would never think of using a statue of the Buddha as an ashtray or the Qur'an as a doorstop but they had been using the altar as a refreshment stand or stand for an overhead projector.

He recalled that there had been complaints from Muslim inmates that they could not get to the prayer room on Fridays, but also that a parallel request had been expressed long before this by Catholics who wanted to go to Mass on Saturday nights and who had been told that they could go on Wednesdays. He did not feel this was a big problem, but the normal time of worship is Saturday evening, and he was dismayed that it seemed to be assumed that they should be happy to be allowed to go at all, regardless of the day and time.

Lawyers and the courts

Prayer facilities

A female, African-Caribbean, legal advisor reported that a number of appeal courts in her area now have a consultation room allocated as a multi-faith prayer room, and those using the room may be asked to leave if it is needed for prayer or worship. Like many others in the course of the local interviews, she noted that accommodating such needs does not require going to enormous lengths and that small actions can be greatly appreciated.

Training of lawyers and judges

One interviewee raised a point about the socialization process law students undergo as part of their education. She explained that when students dine with barristers, the student sitting in a particular seat has the responsibility for standing up and asking for permission to smoke. One day, it was the turn of a Muslim woman wearing a hijab. The interviewee felt that this was in itself highly ironic, given that Muslim women do not smoke. Usually, in response to the request to smoke, the judge declines the request and makes the student argue their case that they should be allowed to smoke – but in this case this did not happen. The interviewee saw this as different treatment in a variety of ways, including a divergence from a normal practice that was designed to help students develop confidence and argumentation skills. She felt that in the legal profession there is an ethos of "conform first, worry about yourself later."

A male, Sikh, race equality representative drew attention to the training of judges that is currently taking place with regards both to racism and the implementation of the Human Rights Act.

Finding solutions

The most common suggestions made by respondents to the postal survey were:

- policy reviews in each service area to promote equal treatment
- better training of staff
- public education programmes/improved awareness
- changes in law.

Other suggestions included: increased consultation, more minority representation, greater flexibility and acceptance of religious customs, recognition of groups as legitimate, and monitoring and reform of the *Prison Act*.

Immigration

Because of ancestral origins outside of the United Kingdom, some religious minorities have much more experience of the immigration system than the population at large. Those who have not been immigrants or asylum seekers themselves may still have come into contact with the system through the experiences of family members or others in the community. For some traditions the visits of religious leaders from abroad have also raised issues about the immigration system.

Findings from the questionnaire survey

More than three quarters of the Muslim organisations answering the questions in this section stated that immigration staff, policies and practices were all sources of unfair treatment. Most of these organisations said the unfairness was 'frequent' rather than occasional.

Around two thirds of Sikh and Hindu organisations also found unfairness in the immigration system, with staff attitudes being mentioned more often than policy and practice. Although there were only a handful of NRM, Zoroastrian and inter-faith responses, the majority of these also said their members experienced unfair treatment.

Many Christian traditions indicated little or no experience of unfair treatment in this area, but there were exceptions – in particular, the black-led organisations.

Unfair treatment from the immigration system: quotes from the postal survey

Bahá'í: *"difficulty with entry visas"*, *"problems obtaining residency"*

Buddhist: *"delays"*

Christian: *"treated as a criminal"*, *"entry to Britain made hard"*

Hindus: *"deported when trying to attend Hindu wedding"*, *"barriers to priest coming from India"*, *"refusal of visa to priest"*

Inter-faith: *"bonding scheme"*, *"difficult to get visa"*, *"members refused entry"*, *"missionaries not recognised"*

Muslims: *"government bond scheme for visitor"*, *"refused visas"*

NRMs/Pagans: *"refused entry to country"*

Sikhs: *"did not allow visa"*

Zoroastrians: *"visa not allowed"*, *"colour and ethnicity"*

Local interviews
Arranged marriages

A female African-Caribbean legal advice/advocacy representative noted the problems arising from differing cultural and religious values and traditions in respect of the tests of genuineness that are conducted as part of entry clearance procedures for those wishing to enter this country in order to marry:

> ...people abiding by a code of behaviour which is strange to an [immigration] agent could result in applications [for bringing spouses into the country] being lost.

She noted that a line of questioning often used was to the effect that:

If there was no courtship, then why did you marry?...you hardly know anything about this person.

This was felt to reflect a complete lack of understanding and/or acceptance of the nature of arranged marriage. Other cultural issues may also have a bearing on decisions too, such as the fact that Hindus might first have a civil marriage ceremony, but will not live together until the religious ceremony has been performed. Due to the need to determine an auspicious time for such an event, the religious ceremony may only take place some considerable time later.

Visas

A number of organisations from different religious traditions said they had experienced difficulties in obtaining visas for visiting religious leaders. A Buddhist interviewee said it is difficult to get sufficient visas for the number of monks needed to come to live and teach in the United Kingdom. Although monks are typically allowed six month holiday visas, it is hard to get permission for them to stay for the two to three years which would be more appropriate for their effective transition to this country and for the work that they need to do within it. Short stays were seen as being disruptive of both the foundations of the Buddhist community and of religious practice within it.

We have fought individually and collectively through Parliament to be able to get a visa for one monk, yet it depends upon luck, rather than a consistent procedure or a right to have them.

Moreover, he noted that cultural and religious assumptions embodied in the framing of legislation created difficulties for religions that understood and constructed themselves in ways different to the majority Christian community. For example, in respect of the Buddhist community's need for monks:

...the law says they must be 'ministers of religion' – monks are not such – this is not an equivalent term, but we must call them as such.

This interviewee recommended having a 'Chief Monk' for the United Kingdom who could determine how many visiting monks were needed and could then liaise with the Government on such matters.

Asylum seekers

A number of interviewees were concerned that current policies for the dispersal of asylum seekers tends to locate them away from the places where they might find appropriate cultural and religious support networks, including places of worship. It was also noted that the food voucher system did not properly accommodate the needs of those Muslim asylum-seekers who require halal food.

Finding solutions

The suggestions made by respondents to the postal survey were similar to those made in respect of the criminal justice system, focusing in particular on:

- policy reviews in each service area to promote equal treatment
- better training of staff
- public education programmes/improved awareness.

6   Housing and planning

Religious 'use' needs to be seen as any other legitimate planning use or need, and must be given the same rigorous analysis rather than assuming that 'oh, religion, here comes a problem'.
(A planner from a Sikh background)

Housing is both a major consumer good and a basic human need. The home is the centre of family life but it also brings people into contact with neighbours and communities. Concepts of space, belonging and territory come into play. Religion and culture can affect housing needs and preferences; and people's views about what facilities should or should not be provided in the neighbourhood.

Findings from the questionnaire survey

- Around two thirds of Muslim organisations reported frequent or occasional unfair treatment from the staff, policies and practices of private landlords, local authorities and housing associations, and about half reported unfair treatment from estate agents.
- Similarly high proportions of Sikh and Hindu organisations picked out private landlords, but they were less likely than Muslims to identify unfair treatment from the two types of social landlord.
- Christian, Jewish, Buddhist and Bahá'í organisations were less likely to identify unfair treatment in housing than Muslims, Sikhs and Hindus. In addition, fewer of the former organisations felt that their members were unfairly treated in housing than they were in education or employment.
- Organisations from most religions were more likely to identify private landlords as a source of unfair treatment than estate agents or social landlords.
- In each tenure, more organisations from almost every religious tradition picked neighbours or other tenants as a source of unfair treatment than picked agencies involved in the provision of housing.
- Fewer than one in ten Christian organisations identified unfair treatment from policy or practice in any housing tenure.
- Some Christian traditions reported little or no unfair treatment in any aspect of housing. Black-led organisations and those in the Christian (other) category were the most likely to indicate that their members experienced problems.

- Over half of Muslim and Hindu organisations identified unfair treatment by planners and unfairness in planning policy and practice, compared with around one in five Christian organisations. Amongst the latter, organisations in the black-led, Pentecostal and 'other' traditions were more likely to report unfairness than other denominations.

Unfair treatment in housing and planning: quotes from the postal survey

Hindus: *"make excuses", "language", "planning permission", "poor location", "verbal abuse", "placed in bad neighbourhoods"*

Inter-faith: *"verbal abuse", "problems during festivals", "racial harassment"*

Muslims: *"get small house", "verbal abuse", "bad housing location", "given unwanted housing", "overcrowding", "housing policy not equal", "not provide housing benefit", "offer withdrawn for being Muslim", "lack of representation in council", "biased attitude", "ethnic cleansing", "festivals and customs", "tenants badly treated", "rarely given grants", "planning authority is full of racists", "application to extend mosque rejected",*

NRMs/Pagans: *"bullying", "biased attitude", "negative attitudes", "removal of religious symbols", "verbal abuse", "refusal to admit the sacredness of a place"*

Sikhs: *"ignorance", "lack of equal opportunity", "discrimination", "verbal and written abuse", "lack of respect", "disputes over fences and parking", "planners unsympathetic to needs"*

Local interviews

The interviews elicited contributions on housing that were often more about racism than specific issues of religious belief and practice. However, one issue particularly raised by both Hindus and Muslims of South Asian background, and which is both cultural and religious, is the need for larger housing that can accommodate extended and inter-generational family groups.

Planning issues were primarily raised by interviewees in the context of discussions about permission for places of worship. Planning concerns can be especially significant for minority communities since the adaptation of existing buildings or the construction of new ones for religious purposes involves issues of "place", "territory" and change in the neighbourhood landscape. "Newcomers" are seen to be "making their mark" through the acquisition and use of public space. Buildings that have a religious purpose are charged with symbolic meanings, not only for those who use them, but also for others within the neighbourhood.

Territories, tensions and "turf wars"

Sometimes, areas that have a reputation for racism are areas that have been the focus of decades or even centuries of immigration and turnover. In such areas there can be a tendency for people to assert that because the area has been so diverse for so long, people are very tolerant or that there is "no problem" with discrimination.

Interviewees commented that the attitudes and approach of estate agents seemed to contribute to the devaluation of property in areas with substantial minority ethnic populations. The consequence of this was seen to be greater polarisation and a de facto "segregation" of different communities. This was, in turn, seen as further reinforcing an environment in which racism and antagonism can flourish. As a police inspector put it:

> ...the less people know about each other the more problems, especially regarding issues of race which are so emotive and because race and religion go hand in hand, making things even more polarised...

This inspector also felt that the greater the segregation and polarisation of communities, the harder it was to shift negative attitudes and behaviour. However, it should also be noted that the assertion of "no problem here" is also made with regard to areas that are apparently more ethnically or culturally homogenous. In these areas, one encounters the argument that because there is little diversity (in other words because there are fewer members of the local community who might be considered "outsiders" or "different") there is no basis upon which intolerance would have been cultivated.

Several interviewees pointed out that there were less instances of vandalism in areas where there was greater geographical "segregation" of different communities, but that the "border" areas between such neighbourhoods were often the focus for significant tensions.

Neighbours and disputes

In contrast to respondents to the postal survey, interviewees did not report many instances of personal conflicts between neighbours on the basis of religion. However, one example cited included a dispute between two neighbours which, whilst it did not originate as a religious conflict, ended up involving religious insults and tensions as the conflict unfolded. This dispute began when a woman began to open up her home to prostitutes in the area so they could stop and have a cup of tea. Despite being friendly with this woman for years, her Muslim neighbours objected to the presence of the prostitutes and to her support for them. As the conflict developed, the woman began to put ceramic statuettes of pigs in her front window in order to cause deliberate offence to her Muslim neighbours. The younger members of the Muslim family then retaliated by causing damage to the woman's property. Eventually, those involved agreed to mediation in order to end the dispute.

A mediation advisor pointed out that neighbourhood conflicts usually arise due to differences in lifestyles:

> During Ramadan, for example, non-Muslims mightn't understand why people are out in the streets all night. There are noise issues associated with African-Caribbean youths, problems between whites and Asians stemming from cooking smells, and late night noise due to visiting. There are also Muslim-Hindu tensions...Differences in lifestyle are, in turn, exacerbated by growing lack of relationships between neighbours, increasing anonymity, and fast turnover of residents. These instabilities make things like noise seem worse.

Several mediation advisers endorsed this perspective and also emphasised how crucial the link was between poverty, disadvantage and social exclusion in the creation of disharmony within and among neighbourhoods.

From spires to minarets

One interviewee noted that there are quite a number of people in the majority community who are "mourning the passing of a Christian landscape, but they're not taking a pluralistic view". The superimposing of new architectures and ownership upon territories that were previously part of a Church of England parish landscape can run into a "NIMBY" response:

> ...people have fears about religion, about change, especially if you come in and change the neighbourhood.

A variety of issues and concerns can also become attached to debates around the buildings themselves. For example, in one place, local opposition to what was to become a Hindu temple centred upon claims about "cooking smells". This was before anyone had moved into the building and certainly before anything was cooked. It also did not take account of the fact that, in its cooking, the religious group concerned uses neither onions or garlic, and only a few spices.

Planning procedures can also cause immense frustration to religious communities who are seeking to establish a place of worship. In one example, an interviewee pulled out a stack of photocopied letters and commented that "people come out of nowhere to object". In this case, nobody from the immediate area was opposing the application, and the individual who initially set up opposition to it lives half a mile away. One group noted that:

> ...once petitions go around, councillors and MPs side with the mainstream community and the temple has no chance.

Perceived inconsistencies in planning policy and practice

Neighbourhood traffic and parking issues are often cited by planning departments as a reason for rejecting planning applications for places of worship. In response to this, one interviewee asked, "what about the football stadium?". In relation to noise problems, the same individual said "but what about the noise from the pub next door which is open much later than the temple?".

Both Hindu and Muslim interviewees pointed out that ringing of church bells does not seem to be regarded as a problem, yet great restrictions are placed on the public broadcasting of the Muslim call to prayer.

A Buddhist vihara based in a house, and which put up a gate without first obtaining planning permission, received a visit from the local authority. As a result of this visit, the vihara was also told to take down a small relief sculpture that was attached to the side of house on the grounds that it was a religious symbol.

A number of interviewees found it difficult to understand why it can sometimes seem easier to obtain permission to convert old church buildings into residential flats than to change them into a place of worship for another religion. A Hindu said that thirty years or so ago there seemed to be less difficulty than now. He thought that this was possibly due to fears of community expansion.

When permissions are granted, other planning decisions in the immediate area can seem to be made without regard to the presence of the religious building. This can result in what, perhaps, should have been seen as foreseeable problems. An example was given in which:

> The Council gave permission for a mosque, but then gave permission for a night club next door, and later a gay/lesbian club. This was not just a matter of religious beliefs....it was hard to have little children around for evening activities and lessons as people around the area were often drunk, shouting, and abusive.

Vandalism and places of worship

Interviewees gave several examples of graffiti and vandalism of cemeteries and places of worship. Hindu interviewees explained that at one temple there had been damage to the cars of devotees and that, despite security arrangements, some worshippers had been physically attacked when seeking to attend the temple at festival times. In another instance, a mosque had had to be kept boarded up for security. However, it was often acknowledged that the problems of vandalism were possibly more the result of general anti-social behaviour rather than of specific targeting on the basis of religion. According to a victim support worker:

> ...most victims see them as opportunist crimes and do not identify them as the result of harassment on the basis of religion.

Problems of this kind can also affect Christian churches. One congregation had purchased an old hall and had problems with a neighbouring pub manager with whom they shared a car park. Every time that church members congregated in front of the door bordering on the car park, the pub manager claimed that they should not be using it and rang the police, despite the local authority having given permission for such use. In this case, following police intervention, the problems were resolved to the satisfaction of all involved. Also in this case, neighbouring Muslim storeowners had at first also not liked the presence of the church, but gradually became reconciled to this because of the additional custom from churchgoers.

A white, female mediation worker noted that, if the tensions and conflicts arising from such issues are to be tackled, then things other than the presenting issues need to be engaged with:

> ... the fundamental premise is that underneath the surface of neighbourhood conflicts or turf battles are unmet needs, fears. Someone saying "you can't build mosque here" could also be more about the fact that their friends have moved away, and they have unmet needs stemming from belonging issues.

Finding solutions

Respondents to the postal survey were asked to suggest ways in which unfair treatment in housing and planning could be tackled. The main suggestions were:

- public education programmes and improved awareness
- policy reviews to promote equal treatment
- changes in law
- more consultation.

Other suggestions included: the need to employ staff from the same religion, better training for staff, monitoring, more flexibility in service provision, independent assessment and voluntary codes of practice.

Interviewees thought that planning policies were inconsistent from one local authority area to the next. Some policies take explicit account of religious dimensions and needs. Others do not focus on religious needs as such, but recognise the need for accessible religious buildings as part of a more general set of criteria for the population and the locality. One planning authority had an informal code of practice in which, in return for taking account of religious needs as part of overall community needs, places of worship are asked to give appropriate notice of when a festival is coming up.

A Sikh planner noted that "*a use is a use*". His authority has tried to create an entire package of measures to relate to religious communities and organisations in which there is an explicit policy with regard to places of worship; translators are provided; assistance is given in preparing effective planning proposals; and communities have been assisted to locate appropriate buildings. This planner expressed the conviction that:

> Religious "use" needs to be seen as any other legitimate planning use or need, and must be given the same rigorous analysis rather than assuming that "oh, religion, here comes a problem".

In his view, the way forward must be to "mainstream" religious use and needs as part of an overall planning policy rather than continuing to marginalise or make a problem out of religion by "*adding it on*" to other issues. One local authority worker felt that the council "must be bold" in pursuing such an approach since, if religion is not incorporated into the mainstream policy, then there is a likelihood that planning issues connected with religion "*won't be dealt with in a coherent manner*". However, the person concerned also noted that no "quick fix" was available here either, since developing such a coherent policy can take between ten and fifteen years.

A representative of one Gurdwara, however, thought that a great deal of the responsibility for what happens with these issues lies with the religious communities themselves. He reported that his own Gurdwara had taken a range of initiatives to minimise potential problems for the surrounding neighbourhood. For example, they have designated someone to monitor the cars and to notify relevant people of any car parking problems or other trouble. They have also posted signs throughout the Gurdwara reminding people to take particular care in parking responsibly. And, like many other places of worship, they are open to the wider community, often inviting people into the Gurdwara so that local residents can get to know them better.

Health care and social services

...the younger generation know how to fight, to speak, they know the requirements. We tell them the elders' requirements so they know whether or not they follow them themselves.
(A Hindu interviewee on the mediating role that youth can play)

The religious identities of individuals and communities can give rise to distinctive needs and patterns of behaviour. Some of the issues that need to be recognised and addressed by providers of health care and social services are extremely sensitive and complex – for example, suicide, domestic violence, death and burial.

Findings from the questionnaire survey

NHS surgeries and health centres

Sikh organisations were the most likely to identify unfair treatment at NHS surgeries and health centres, with around two out of three reporting unfair treatment of their members by medical and non-medical staff. However, nearly all these organisations said the unfair treatment was 'occasional' rather than 'frequent'. This figure of two out three compares with 10-20 per cent of Christian organisations, although the proportion was higher for organisations belonging to the black-led and 'other' categories than for other Christian traditions.

In nearly all religious traditions, fewer organisations recorded unfair treatment from the policies and practices of health centres and surgeries than from the attitudes and behaviour of staff.

NHS Hospitals

Asked about NHS hospital staff, patients, policies and practices, organisations from the Sikh, Muslim, Christian and Hindu traditions were most likely to indicate that staff were a source of unfair treatment, and least likely to pick out policy.

Around two thirds of Sikh organisations and over half of Muslim organisations recorded unfair treatment from NHS staff. A majority of the small number of responses from NRM/Pagan, Zoroastrian and inter-faith organisations did the same. Muslims were the most likely to say that the unfairness was 'frequent' rather than 'occasional'. Little or no unfair treatment in any aspect of NHS health care was reported by Buddhist organisations.

Private health care

Fewer organisations were in a position to answer questions about private health care. In most religions, the organisations that did offer views on this were less likely to indicate unfair treatment from staff and practices in the private system than in the NHS.

Examples of unfair treatment in health care

Specific examples of unfair treatment that were given by respondents included the following:

- Chaplaincy and facilities for worship (Muslims, NRM/Pagans and inter-faith)
- Dietary needs (Jains, Muslims, Sikhs, and inter-faith)
- Language barriers (Sikhs, inter-faith)
- Medical techniques (Jains, Muslims, Christians).

Unfair treatment in health care: quotes from the postal survey

Jains: *"medication tested on animals"*

Muslims: *"elderly overlooked"*, *"unsuitable medicines"*, *"female doctor for women patients"*, *"lack of attention"*, *"proper care not given by GPs"*, *"doctor not responsive to needs"*, *"circumcision not available"*, *"no Muslims at higher levels"*, *"stereotyping female mental patient"*, *"Muslims ignored"*, *"impolite staff"*, *"post-death and female requirements"*

NRMs/Pagans: *"Pagan not listed on forms"*, *"categorised as C of E"*, *"verbal abuse"*, *"hospital refuses donations from our religion"*, *"medical staff are suspicious and biased"*

Sikhs: *"hair removal"*, *"will not remove 5 K's"*, *"GPs don't care for elderly"*

Social services

Around three quarters of Muslim organisations reported unfair treatment from social services staff and from practices in social services departments. The majority of NRM/Pagan organisations answering questions on social services did likewise. The corresponding figure for Christian organisations was around one in five, but was higher for black-led, Pentecostal, Presbyterian and Christian organisations in the 'other' category.

The responses from virtually all religions suggest that there is a perceived gap between policy and practice in social services, with more organisations indicating occasional unfair treatment from the latter than the former.

Unfair treatment in social services: quotes from the postal survey

Hindus: *"they should cater for Asian religions"*

Jains: *"no awareness of Jain community"*

Muslims: *"child adopted by non-Muslims"*, *"children placed with non Muslims"*, *"complaints ignored to protect staff"*, *"social workers caused misery"*

NRMs/Pagans: *"fostering made difficult"*, *"child taken away for being a witch"*, *"Pagans treated with hostility and mistrust"*, *"accused of being devil worshipers"*, *"diet"*

Sikhs: *"less support to disabled/elderly"*

Local interviews

Health care, as such, was not a major focus of the local interviews. However, a number of discussions with hospital chaplains took place during the course of fieldwork and other interviewees sometimes referred to health care issues.

Food and clothing in hospitals

In one location Hindus experienced difficulties when family members were not allowed to bring their own food into the hospital. They had wished to do this because, for the more elderly and devout patients, the hospital's standard vegetarian meals were not felt to be appropriate. It was also noted that many women did not feel comfortable wearing the hospital standard nightdress during the daytime and preferred to wear their saris. The local religious community was very active in contacting the hospital to explain these issues and, as a result, the need for specific interventions had gradually decreased.

Burials and cremations

A number of concerns were reported around death and burial. These included instances where coroners and/or medical staff have refused to allow Muslims access to prepare the body of the deceased, despite the provisions of the Coroners Act which allow for exemptions. An interviewee commented that one can *"issue proceedings, habeas corpus, etc, but by that time it's too late"*.

A group of Buddhists also noted difficulties in connection with arrangements for the deceased and felt that there should be a co-ordinator in hospitals who can contact community members to provide the appropriate rites.

After much pressure, a local Hindu community persuaded the local authority to build a crematorium, and themselves contributed financial resources. However, there was still felt to be unfair treatment because Christian scriptures and religious symbols were provided in the prayer room attached to the crematorium, whilst Hindus and others were asked to supply their own.

Circumcision

For Jews and Muslims, issues connected with circumcision of male children can sometimes give rise to problems. It was noted that the availability of the operation on the NHS varies from one area to another. Interviewees noted that *"in England, we have a black economy"* of unlicensed GPs who do the procedure without proper insurance or authority.

Blood-based treatments

For Jehovah's Witnesses there are significant difficulties related to their refusal, on religious grounds, to accept blood-based treatments. They reported that, because of this, they are stigmatised as *"martyrs"* and *"children murderers"* and are sometimes seen as *"having a death wish"*. A representative stated:

> *If it involves children, it can become a major legal issue under the Child Protection Act. Yet you look at the dangers other parents put their children under in all sorts of other "normal, everyday life" contexts like poor housing and living environment, but those don't have the stigma of being child murderers.*

Chaplaincy services

A number of issues were identified in respect of organised support for religious and spiritual needs in hospitals. The provisions for chaplaincy and spiritual needs vary considerably from hospital to hospital, depending upon a variety of factors such as demographics, the size of hospital, and the resources available. Religious minorities have not had the tradition of privileged access that has more traditionally been available to Christian chaplains. In this context, one chaplain drew attention to the complex problems connected with representation of minority religions on the regulatory bodies responsible for hospital chaplaincy.

Some issues were reported even in respect of traditional Christian chaplaincy work. For example, attention was drawn to a recent development in which, on the grounds of the Data Protection Act, one hospital no longer allows Roman Catholic Christian clergy to come in and enquire about which patients are Catholic in order to arrange to visit them.

Residential care

Needs were especially identified in the context of care for the elderly, where it was reported that there was often a lack of knowledge of, and sensitivity to, religious and cultural requirements. This applied to Asian elderly people in particular, but to others as well. For example, when an elderly Jehovah's Witness woman spat out the coffee that she had been given, she was labelled "anti-social", although the drinking of coffee was forbidden by her religion.

In at least one of the local areas, however, significant advances had been made in trying to meet the needs of elderly members of ethnic and religious minorities within both elderly residential and youth care.

Other social services issues

Some institutional interventions with regard to religious minorities arouse great sensitivity on all sides. Examples are female circumcision/genital mutilation, depression, suicide and domestic violence. Particularly difficult in relation to some of these matters is the question of who should be consulted; of who represents who; and of who should decide what. A number of interviewees recognised the sensitivity of some of the issues involved, but also expressed concerns about "disguising abuse under a religious guise", especially in relation to instances of domestic abuse and child abuse. A white, female, local authority officer cited an example of a women's shelter, established in response to a growing number of suicides, which was vigorously opposed by Asian representatives of various religious traditions.

Another example cited by a white, male, local authority officer involved a controversy over the provision of appropriate services to Kosovan refugees. The local Muslim community wanted to respond to these needs as an expression of religious solidarity. They therefore approached the local authority with representations about what should happen. The local authority, however, wanted to wait to establish the needs of the Kosovans through direct consultation with them, rather than through representations on their behalf by local Muslims. Such examples illustrate some of the difficult dilemmas involved in terms of representation and legitimacy.

Finding solutions

The main suggestions made by respondents to the postal survey were:

For tackling unfair treatment in health care
- Public education programmes and improved awareness
- Better training for staff
- More consultation between staff and patients.

Other suggestions included policy reviews, changes in the law, more ethnic minority representation in senior positions, better monitoring, improving facilities, and voluntary codes of practice.

And in the social services
- Staff training
- Policy reviews in each area to promote equal treatment
- More consultation

Other suggestions included public education programmes and changes in the law.

Hospital chaplaincy
A number of hospitals in the case study areas had tried to accommodate the changing religious profile of the local populations. For example, in one case there is now a multi-faith prayer room. However, it was also reported that this room had been vandalised and that a copy of the Qur'an had been desecrated. In the light of this experience, the room has

recently been redesigned, with the installation of high shelves for storage, a video camera outside the door for security, and a no smoking/no eating sign. The room is now locked at night.

A Christian chaplain said he felt hospitals should be proactive and that they should apply for outside funding to develop their services. His hospital had set up various partnerships with lay religious organisations. He was also working to expand the role and composition of pastoral volunteers, in order to overcome the perception that such roles have a Christian and/or evangelical purpose.

Liaison and involvement

At an international level there have been initiatives led by the medical profession to develop treatments that are not blood-based and that would be acceptable to Jehovah's Witnesses. An interviewee from this tradition explained that he understood the difficulties faced by doctors, both in terms of their concerns about possible legal liability if they do not provide blood-based treatments, and because they feel that not giving blood hinders their ability to help a patient.

At the local level, Jehovah's Witnesses have often taken the initiative in establishing hospital liaison committees. These have been established in order to encourage consideration of what alternatives are available. It was explained that, in this way, the Jehovah's Witnesses:

> ... are trying to inform the medical community what they can/can't do as far as Jehovah's Witnesses are concerned. They have a list of surgeons who perform bloodless operations...

In addition, as a way of contributing something to the wider community the Jehovah's Witnesses have, in one locality, donated cell salvage machines to the local hospital.

With regard to the religious minorities that are primarily composed of people of South Asian minority ethnic origins, a Hindu interviewee noted that the youth of the community can sometimes play a useful mediating role:

> ...the younger generation know how to fight, to speak, they know the requirements. We tell them the elders' requirements so they know whether or not they follow them themselves.

8   Public transport, shops and leisure

The postal questionnaire (see annex A) contained short sections on public transport, local authority leisure services, and shops and stores. These issues were not covered to any extent in the local interviews.

The proportion of organisations from each religion reporting unfair treatment of their members in these three areas was generally lower than that for other services, with most organisations saying that the unfairness was 'occasional' rather than 'frequent'.

Public transport

- More than one in three Hindu, Muslim and Sikh organisations reported unfair treatment of their members from public transport staff.
- Fewer organisations from these religions reported problems with the policies and practices of transport providers
- Most other religious traditions reported little or no unfair treatment on public transport.

Local authority leisure services

- Nearly two thirds of Muslim organisations and a third of Hindu and Sikh organisations said their members experienced unfair treatment from staff in leisure services departments.
- A similar proportion of organisations from these religions reported unfairness in policy and practice.
- Very few Christian, Buddhist or Bahá'í organisations reported unfair treatment in these areas.

Shops and stores

- Between a third and a half of Hindu, Muslim and Sikh organisations reported unfair treatment from staff, customers, or the policies and practices of shops and stores.
- The equivalent proportions for other traditions were lower – for example, fewer than one in ten Christian organisations (although the proportions were higher for the handful black-led Christian organisations responding to the questionnaire).

Unfair treatment: quotes from the postal survey

Public transport
Muslims: *"women forced to unveil for ID"*

Leisure services
Muslims: *"unfair treatment from sports centres", "no single sex swimming"*

NRM/Pagans: *"difficulty hiring halls"*

Sikhs: *"banned from wearing Kirpan"*

Shops and stores
Inter-faith: *"it is a problem of racism not religion", "access to pub facilities", "experienced unfair treatment on market stall"*

Muslims: *"stores do not cater for diet", "failure to grant planning permission"*

Sikhs: *"general attitude", "misunderstanding'*

There is a need to ensure the equitable distribution of resources, without having to play games; then perceptions will change.
An interviewee

Funding – whether it is obtained from public donation, charities, or local or central government sources – is clearly an issue that is of concern to religious organisations themselves, and they were therefore asked to respond to the postal questionnaire on behalf of their organisations rather than their members. They were also asked, however, about the experiences of their members with the Benefits Agency.

Findings from the questionnaire survey

Many organisations did not have sufficient experience of applying for funds to answer these questions. Because of the small numbers, not all religious traditions have been included in this analysis.

Funding of organisations

- Around half the Hindu and Muslim organisations in the survey reported that they experienced frequent or occasional unfair treatment from charity staff and from the policies and practices of charities. For Christian, Jewish and Buddhist organisations the equivalent proportion was generally less than one in four.
- Organisations from nearly all the above traditions were more likely to report that they experienced unfair treatment from local government (for example, about two thirds of the Muslim and half to two thirds of the Hindu and Sikh organisations).
- Fewer organisations had experience of applying for funding from central government. Of those that did, the proportions reporting unfair treatment were similar to those for local government.
- Over half of the Muslim, Hindu and Sikh, but less than a quarter of the Christian, Jewish or Buddhist organisations said they experienced unfair treatment from the attitudes or behaviour of the public when seeking donations. However, compared with charity and government funding, Muslim and Sikh

organisations were much more likely to report that unfairness from the public was 'occasional' rather than 'frequent'.

- The 7-10 black-led organisations answering these questions were more likely to report unfair treatment in every aspect of funding than the other Christian traditions.
- There was some variation between organisations from the six traditions as to whether staff, policy or practice were the most frequent source of unfair treatment, although all were slightly more likely to indicate unfairness from local government practices than local government policies.

Specific examples of unfair treatment mentioned by respondents included the following:

- general lack of funding for religious organisations (Hindus, inter-faith, Muslims, NRMs/Pagans, Sikhs)
- lack of recognition/knowledge of faith/religious organisations (inter-faith, Muslims, NRM/Pagans, Sikhs, Zoroastrians)
- unfair bias in policies (Hindus, inter-faith, Muslims, NRMs/Pagans, Zoroastrians)
- application procedures (inter-faith, Muslims, Zoroastrians)
- attitudes and behaviour of the general public (Muslims).

Benefits

About half the Muslim, Sikh and Hindu organisations who answered this question stated that their members experienced unfair treatment from Benefits Agency staff, with the large majority saying that this was occasional rather than frequent. A smaller proportion said that the policies and practices of the agency were unfair. Other religious traditions were less likely to report unfair treatment from this source.

Local interviews

Issues of funding were raised in a variety of contexts, particularly in interviews with religious individuals and representatives of religious organisations. They were also discussed with staff associated with relevant local authority departments.

Exclusion from funding

Within the Christian tradition, inequities can be experienced by non-Established Christian denominations. For example, several Christian clergy of various denominations noted that Church of England cathedrals received money for improvements from the local authority, whereas other Christian churches and places of worship do not seem to do so. It was accepted that Anglican cathedrals are often located in the town centre and may be seen as buildings of wider "public interest", or even as tourist sites. However, a representative of the Roman Catholic Church reported that even though their own cathedral was one of the major sites in the city centre, it was not treated equitably in comparison with a Church of England cathedral.

In the experience of a number of interviewees, local authorities often do not fund applications from religious organisations who wish to develop local services for the wider public, on the basis that public money should not support a particular religion. The difficulty with this approach is that places of worship very often function as "hubs", infrastructures, and a basis for resources and services that are intended to be of benefit to the wider community. In the view of the interviewees who raised this issue, applications from groups who present themselves in primarily ethnic or cultural terms are more likely to succeed.

The attempt by local authorities to distinguish religion from culture was reported by a number of interviewees to have been applied inconsistently. Festivals, for example, were said to be a particular problem, although one local authority officer acknowledged that they could be both cultural and religious:

> Christmas may be celebrated by many who mightn't see it as a holy day. Diwali might be religious in a sense, but may be seen more as a cultural celebration.

Another noted that it is:

> ...rare to receive an application solely on the basis of a religious celebration or activity. We get a lot for cultural celebrations associated with religion but usually they are clearly cultural enough so as to be able to fund them...The biggest issue is getting groups to be accountable for expenditure.

Inconsistency in funding decisions was often cited as being a significant factor in exacerbating cross-community tensions and negative attitudes among organisations and communities that are already competing for scarce resources.

It was said that in order to get around the barriers to local authority funding, a number of organisations have effectively been forced to call themselves "community" or "cultural" centres rather than indicating the religious basis for their activities. Yet for many, such a "trade off" is too costly a price to pay. It is felt to entail a bargaining away of their core identity and it contributes to their invisibility within the local religious and wider community landscape, which in turn contributes to their continuing marginalisation. Moreover a number of people were concerned that presenting one's organisation in such ways might amount to being dishonest in order to gain funding. This was, in turn, felt to be putting them into a position which could violate the ethical basis and content of their religious belief and practice.

Funding and equal opportunities requirements

Even when religious organisations obtain funding to provide community services, other difficulties can emerge. One example of this was that of a multi-purpose, Christian community centre which provides activities and services for elderly people and youth as well as space for other groups. The staff of the centre are generally committed to equalities as part of their Christian belief. However, a member of the centre's staff who had been involved in campaigning activities in relation to the provisions of Section 28 of the Local Government Act wrote a letter to a newspaper which might be interpreted as being anti-gay and lesbian.

A white, male, staff member said the centre was then approached by the council asking them *hypothetically* if they would accommodate Qur'an classes and lesbian assertiveness groups on their site (these groups had not actually requested use of the centre). Upon informing the local authority that the centre could not allow these uses of its premises, funding was cut, and many services that had been critical to one of the most disadvantaged communities in the area suffered as a result. The staff member felt that this reflected a growing secular, and especially anti-Christian, sentiment. He felt that, if the Council had taken a similar approach to a Muslim organisation or a minority ethnic organisation, then this would have been considered racist. In his view the action taken against his own centre actually amounted to:

> ...discrimination against white Christian organisations under the guise of equal opportunities.

He also expressed scepticism about how many South Asian centres employ non-South Asian staff, and drew attention to what he felt to be a "selective application" of equal opportunities policies, which he perceived as being to the disadvantage of religious organisations in general and, in this case, specifically to organisations with a Christian basis.

Voluntary sector problems

Difficulties were also reported with regard to the impact upon religious organisations of more general funding policies. In common with many other voluntary sector organisations, they may not have permanent employees with the level of training needed to keep a particular project going after initial and limited funding has been exhausted. The granting of start-up funds without integral provision of capacity-building resources can result in it being impossible for religious organisations to sustain initiatives.

Finding solutions

The most common suggestions made by respondents to the postal survey were:
- policy reviews in each service area to promote equal treatment
- public education programmes and improved awareness
- increasing funding/support for religious groups.

Other suggestions included monitoring of funding allocations, more consultation, greater flexibility and acceptance of religion, voluntary codes of practice, changes in the law, and better staff training.

Some of the local interviewees noted a shift in the focus of funding criteria and decision-making, with less attention being paid to the type of organisation that is seeking to provide the service, and more to the quality, efficiency and appropriateness of the service that is being provided. In this context, it was pointed out that religious organisations are sometimes the only ones in a position to provide services to some marginalised groups. Overall, there was a widespread conviction that:

There is a need to ensure the equitable distribution of resources, without having to play games; then perceptions will change.

If Oxfam makes a contribution it's reported. If the Sikh community makes a contribution, it never gets covered in the media.
(Comment from a Sikh representative)

The mass media of newspapers, television and radio are a powerful and pervasive feature of modern society. This pervasiveness means that they have a significant capacity both to shape and to reflect the perceptions of others, and also to affect self-perceptions.

Findings from the questionnaire survey

This section of the questionnaire asked about the experiences of the organisation and the religious community to which it belonged, rather than its particular membership. Questions about the attitudes and behaviour of journalists, and about the coverage of their religion in the local and national media, were answered by a relatively high proportion of organisations from all religions. Fewer answered questions about the coverage of their own organisations, reflecting less experience in this area.

General comments
- Overall, for every religious tradition, questions about the media tended to attract claims of unfair treatment from more organisations than other areas of the questionnaire. It was also noticeable that relatively more organisations said the unfairness was 'frequent' as opposed to 'occasional'.
- In most traditions, those organisations with enough experience to answer the question were less likely to report unfair coverage of their own organisation in the media than unfair coverage of their religion, or unfairness in the attitudes and behaviour of journalists.
- On the whole, most traditions were more likely to report unfair treatment from the national media than the local, and from television and newspapers as opposed to radio.

Christians

The number of Christian organisations saying they or their religion experienced unfair treatment from the media far exceeded the number reporting unfair treatment of their members in the other areas of life covered in the questionnaire. 75 per cent reported unfair coverage of Christianity on national television, and about a third of these organisations said the unfairness was 'frequent'. 70 per cent or more also complained of unfair treatment from national newspaper coverage, and from both national newspaper and television journalists.

Within the Christian tradition, organisations in the 'Christian (other)' category were the most likely to report unfair treatment in all aspects of the media.

Muslims

The proportion of Muslim organisations reporting unfair treatment from the media was consistently higher even than that for Christian organisations, and also exceeded the proportion of Muslim organisations saying their members experienced unfair treatment in other areas of life. This latter gap was not as pronounced as it was for Christians, however, because Muslim organisations were much more likely than Christians to report unfair treatment in education, employment, immigration and the criminal justice system.

The number of Muslim organisations reporting 'frequent' unfair treatment from national newspaper journalists and national newspaper coverage greatly exceeded the number saying that unfairness was 'occasional' or non-existent. 80 per cent (44 out of 55) Muslim organisations answering the question said that unfair treatment in the way that national newspapers cover their religion was frequent.

Other religions

The proportion of Sikh and Hindu organisations reporting unfair treatment from the media was also high: generally somewhere between that for Muslim and Christian organisations. Jewish, Buddhist and Bahá'í organisations, on the other hand, were less likely to report unfair treatment than these other religions, although the majority still found unfairness in some aspects of the media.

Between 14 and 22 NRM/Pagan organisations answered this set of questions. At least two thirds of these reported unfair coverage of their religion in all branches of the media and they also reported unfair treatment from most types of journalist.

Examples of unfair treatment

Specific examples of unfair treatment by the media that were given by respondents included the following:

- Lack of coverage of specific religions, or religion in general
- Misrepresentation and bias
- Emphasis on the negative aspects of religion
- Ignorance and indifference
- Racial and religious stereotyping
- Offensive material and coverage
- Lack of access to broadcasting licences.

Unfair treatment from the media: quotes from the postal survey

Christians: *"Anti-Christian", "ignorance of views on abortion, contraception and sexuality", "censorship", "failure to consult mainstream views", "seeing Christianity as less valid than ethnic minority faiths", "reporting of the issues around the ordination of women", "representation of views on genetic engineering", "too much political correctness", "ridicule", "stereotyping and old fashioned portrayals of Christianity," "portrayed as fanatics", "name of Jesus used as a swear word".*

Hindus: *"marginalisation", 'misrepresentation', "coverage of festivals and events", 'cost of advertising'.*

Jews: *"Anti-semitic", "ignore non-orthodox Judaism".*

Muslims: *"seen as homophobic", "portrayed as terrorists", "racism in media", 'Muslim women seen as inferior', 'veiled women seen as victims'.*

NRMs/Pagans: *"accusations of being racist", "failure to cover festivals".*

Sikhs: *"coverage of festivals and events", "no programme to promote religion".*

Local interviews

Although the media were not a central feature of the local interviews, individuals and representatives of religious organisations fairly frequently made reference to the pervasive role of the media and to its power to contribute to a negative perception of their religious traditions and communities. References were also made to the media's potential for positive public education where media representatives were prepared to work positively and consult with religious communities and organisations.

Negative images, sensationalism and ridicule

Reflecting a widespread perception among Muslim interviewees, an individual noted that "the media creates a particular obstacle for the Muslim community" in achieving the levels of trust and interaction needed to move toward positive change. He stated that:

> Ever since the Gulf War, Chechnya – people have been portrayed as terrorists. No one ever asks why they became terrorists.

A member of the Hindu community believed that the media "take extremes and generalise to all Hindus". As a result, he reported that children then question parents asking, "why don't we do that?". He felt that reports are often based on "arbitrarily writing without any information, facts, or knowledge". Another Hindu recalled an instance in which the Sai Baba community was included in an article about cults, noting that the journalist's only source had been the Internet. He stated that, whilst he welcomes criticism, journalists should visit and talk to the people concerned, in order to see for themselves.

It was pointed out that the manner in which newspaper articles are written may also help perpetuate inaccurate perceptions about different communities. One young person asked:

> ...why do news headlines have to say "Black/Asian/Muslim male did x" in the headline and never say anything like 'white Christian male did x' ?

A number of interviewees, particularly from those minority religious traditions which are often portrayed in the media as "sects" or "cults", drew attention to the consequences for their lives that can result from negative coverage. A Unificationist observed:

> Why would I go around saying I'm a "Moonie"; it's like saying I'm a leper; even now what people think is so skewed – especially due to the media.

Several interviewees noted that the media often ridicule people who have strong religious beliefs, including those from within the majority Christian community. A Bahá'í observed that:

...the media portrays stereotypical images of religious communities bobbing up and down on Sundays rather than their aspirations and activities.

One Christian clergyman said that the media have "harassed the Church quite mercilessly". A member of an independent church was:

....astonished by the false picture so often painted by the media of Christians and even Jesus, whose name is often used blasphemously.

He added that:

Everyone is allowed to spout their news, but people are affronted when you start talking about being Christian. It's one thing if they don't want to know about it, but when you get to the point where people are gagging every time something about Christianity is mentioned, you have a problem.

Ignoring positive news

Several interviewees commented that the media ignore positive news about their religions. A Sikh representative reported that although Sikhs have given substantial money to relief in Kosovo, they have not received media recognition of this:

If Oxfam makes a contribution it's reported. If the Sikh community makes a contribution, it never gets covered in the media.

A Bahá'í reported that:

... we send articles to the mainstream newspapers, as we've had lots of events locally and nationally. Despite the many wonderful things people are doing, they don't publish much. Often what we send gets printed in the Asian edition of the local paper...People learning to love one another is not "noteworthy".

A member of the Roman Catholic clergy argued that senior leaders *"who are ecclesiastically tremendous, with great knowledge of the Roman Catholic Church and other religions gained through their travels"* are never asked to give their perspectives, although other Christian clergy are regularly invited. He felt that any secular institution with such expertise and profile would be highlighted or included. However, he felt that as Roman Catholic Christians:

> *...we find ourselves in a position where the church and the clergy are consistently sidelined...Never has a Roman Catholic parish, priest, etc been asked to take part in Sunday evening broadcasts. Catholics are no longer beaten up in the streets, but this is yet another critical situation of prejudice. It's institutionalised prejudice, and can't be dressed up as anything else as no one can provide any reason why we are not included.*

Others reported a *"lack of personal curiosity"* in religious issues or activities on the part of media representatives, even though they may be involved in religious affairs programming. This was especially important because, as one person observed:

> *Discrimination only comes through ignorance; if you know [about religious] values and why they're there and how they're useful, that gives a certain credibility; there is something there they should/could learn about, yet authorities are trying to undermine this.*

Religious programming

One interviewee thought that problems related to religious programming seem to involve similar issues to those associated with ethnic minority programming. For example, the programmes are moved from one poor time slot to another, the support facilities are poor, and there is no mention in promotional material. In contrast, a Jewish interviewee expressed the view that, given the comparatively small size of the Jewish population, in relation to his local area and in the country as a whole, there are a comparatively high number of Jewish-related programmes. Yet despite what he summarised as being an *"enormous amount"* of programming, he remarked that *"you would think people would know more, not less about Jews/Judaism"*.

Finding solutions

The most common suggestions made by respondents to the postal survey were:
- better training for staff including journalists
- greater consultation with religious groups
- policy reviews to promote equal treatment.

Other suggestions included public and school education; provide accurate information; more religious representation/coverage; strengthen press complaints commission; voluntary codes of practice; change in law; greater acceptance of other faiths/customs; and monitoring.

Other religious traditions

….what equality people talk about is a sham because they intimate that we're meant to respect all people except Moonies or Jehovah's Witnesses – it's almost like we can't escape.
(comment from a Unificationist)

Many religious communities, groups and organisations themselves have a history of unfair and discriminatory treatment of other religious groups, and especially of those in numerical minorities. This chapter summarises the reported experience of religious organisations in respect of unfair treatment from religious groups other than their own.

Findings from the questionnaire survey

Respondents were asked whether the organisation or its members had experienced unfair treatment from other religious groups[4]. If so, they were asked to state which group(s) were involved and if possible to provide a specific example.

- For many traditions, the proportion of organisations saying they or their members had experienced unfair treatment was broadly similar: between a quarter and a third of the Christian, Buddhist, Hindu, Jewish, Muslim and Bahá'í organisations that answered this question.
- The proportion was a little higher for Sikh and inter-faith organisations, and nearly two thirds of the NRM/Pagan organisations (14 out of 22 respondents) said they were treated unfairly by other religions.
- Amongst Christian traditions, the proportion was much higher for organisations in the Christian (other) category, where 36 out of 49 (nearly three quarters) said they had been treated unfairly by other religious groups.

---

4   Unlike previous sections of the questionnaire, which distinguished between 'frequent; 'occasional' and 'no' unfair treatment, this question invited a simple yes/no response.

Unfair treatment from other religious groups: quotes from the postal survey

Bahá'ís: *"persecution by Iran"*, *"disruption of meetings by Muslims"*, *"being overlooked in general as a religious group"*

Buddhists: *"denial of use of church hall"*, *"rivalry and factionalism between Western Buddhist Orders"*

Christians: *"anti-Catholic material"*, *"verbal abuse against Catholics"*, *"disruption of Independent Church preachers and gatherings"*, *"Christians pretending to be evangelicals"*, *"claimed anti-Christian expressions by Methodists"*, *"hostility to Christians changing denominations"*, *"Black-led churches' members being refused jobs"*, *"unfair comments and exclusion as a result of the practices of hospital and prison chaplaincies". "*

Christian (other): *"untrue publications about the Church of Christ Scientist written by other Christians"*, *"Christ Scientist literature destroyed"*, *"hostility to Jehovah's Witness's particularly public preachers"*, *"refusal of contact by other Christian groups"*, *"the exclusion of the Unification Church and its treatment as a cult"*, *"the expulsion of children from school"*, *"misrepresentation of the Church of Jesus Christ of Latter-day Saints"*, *"anti-Mormon literature"*, *"treated as cult"*, *"targeted by Jehovah's Witnesses for conversion"*, *"the banning of the Grail Church"*

Hindus: *"abusive telephone calls"*, *"denial of access to use of hall because of smell of incense"*

Inter-faith: *"bias in Christian sermons"*, *"exclusion from celebrations by Christians"*, *"aggressive behaviour by Hindus"*, *"destruction of literature and the disruption of meetings"*, *"lack of support from Muslims"*

Jews: *"misunderstanding"*

Muslims: *"Christian objections to an exhibition"*, *"the exclusion of Sufis and 'white' converts"*, *"the circulation of xenophobic literature by Christians"*

NRM/Pagans: *"stereotyping as occultists or satanists"*, *"posters taken down"*, *"car tyres slashed by Christians"*, *"anti-pagan propaganda"*, *"meetings disrupted"*, *"child abuse allegations"*

Sikhs: *"the representation of Sikhs as Hindus"*, *"lack of guidance for non-halal food"*, *"women not being allowed to sing"*, *"violent attacks at school by Muslim pupils"*, *"arson attacks on buildings"*

144 of the organisations responding to the survey named specific religions that they judged to be responsible for unfair treatment of their organisation or its members: there were 207 such mentions altogether. Christians accounted for nearly half of the mentions made of specific religions by both Christians and non-Christians alike. Muslims accounted for about one in five, with fewer mentions of Hindus and Jews. These are the numerically largest religions in England and Wales, so it is hardly surprising that they should feature in this way.

As some of the above quotes imply, organisations in the survey sometimes mentioned groups from within their own religion as the source of unfair treatment. This was especially true of organisations in the 'Christian (other)' category.

Local interviews

Racism and anti-Semitism

A Jewish interviewee reported feeling that, although the level of anti-semitism varies in different locations, it is "*ingrained everywhere – even with country folk who've never seen a Jew*". His view was that this comes both from Church teachings and from the way in which Christianity is taught. One diversity specialist expressed the view that if the Race Relations Act were taken seriously, then "*the Christian Church would be liable for incitement due to its teachings*". Racism was also often reported with respect to attitudes within the historic Christian Church towards Churches composed of a majority of Christians of African-Caribbean heritage.

Religious tensions were in other ways reported as combining with ethnic rivalries. A white, male, police constable reported that, on one occasion:

> ...*after a group of Indian boys went to retrieve an Indian girl who was dating a Pakistani boy, this led to three days of riots.*

The complex relationship between discrimination based on race and that based on religion was illustrated by the story of a Jewish man from the Indian Jewish community that settled in Bombay some hundreds of years ago as a result of a shipwreck. He noted that some of his family look Indian, some middle Eastern. His parents drifted from their religious tradition and migrated to England:

In England, we met with multiple levels of racism: racism from white English people for being Indian, Hindus for being Jewish, Jews ... for being black. Anti-Semitism was rife, but there were also places which had signs reading 'no Irish, no blacks, no dogs' that would have a mezuzah [Jewish symbol] on the door.

An advice worker noted that African refugees and asylum seekers do not always feel welcome at mosques which have predominantly South Asian congregations. Another interviewee noted that: *"there's racial discrimination within ethnic minority people, no less than with whites"*. Some local residents felt that their local authority councillors were only concerned with the interests of their own ethnic/religious communities. This situation can be exacerbated by a tendency for the more established groups to view new groups in the area as a threat.

Conflict within and between religious groups

Quite a number of interviewees associated with religions other than Islam reported difficulties in their relationships with Muslims, and nearly all religious groups mentioned problems in respect of those, in various religions, who could be described as "fundamentalist" or "evangelical" in stance.

Some Christian interviewees said that because of their openness to Islam and other religions, some Muslims considered them to be weak in their religious convictions. They felt they were often treated poorly as a result, and were beginning to feel increasingly defensive.

Tensions can exist between Orthodox and Progressive Jewish communities. A member of a Jewish discussion group drew attention to what he felt to be the negative attitudes and behaviour of Orthodox Jews, feeling that this was a major cause of the discrimination experienced by his section of the wider Jewish community.

Administrators of church or community halls were said to decline the use of their premises to Pagans and members of New Religious Movements because they are seen as "cults". One Pagan noted that the relationship with the Christian community presents *"a very mixed picture"*. He felt that, *"there is constant bombardment regarding the evils of Paganism"* and went on to recall an incident in which a plane crash was attributed to Paganism, noting that *"If it had been another group involved, it would have been considered incitement"*.

Religious conversion

Conversion from one religion to another also proved to be a sensitive subject for individuals, families and communities alike. One woman in the process of converting to Judaism recalled that she had married an Orthodox Jewish man, and that they had lived in various small communities around England and Scotland. She reported that she had become very involved in the synagogue and Jewish community, but never felt completely accepted because of the mandates of Jewish Orthodoxy. If someone asked her about her religion, she said her reaction was different depending on who was asking:

> If it was a non-Jewish person, I could easily say I was Jewish. If it was a Jewish person asking, I felt I couldn't be as direct or say it as easily … or that I was Jewish at all.

A Christian interviewee reported that some women of South Asian backgrounds who adopt Christianity, do so in secret in order to avoid the domestic violence they fear were their conversion to become publicly known. Members of the Jehovah's Witnesses, the Church of Jesus Christ of Latter-Day Saints, and the Unification Church also reported a variety of experiences of being rejected by families, friends and others when they joined their respective religious communities.

On the other hand, a number of interviewees thought that evangelical/conversion-based religions can seem aggressive and cause members of other religions to feel alienated and defensive. A Hindu representative thought the implicit message of such traditions was that their religion is superior. This, he felt, was not only offensive, but also violated the basic Hindu tenet requiring tolerance of all religions. Although they did not necessarily agree with a law against blasphemy, Hindu interviewees felt there should be some protection from the harm done when, in order to gain conversions, another religion is denounced.

The role of secular institutions

Attention was drawn to the way that the agendas of local authorities, service providers and employers are often shaped by the size and demographics of their surrounding populations. As a consequence, initiatives can tend to focus on issues pertaining to the "majority-minority" communities rather than dealing with diversities across the full range of different traditions and communities. This can result in a tendency to address the needs of the Muslim community first, leaving the particulars associated with other minority religions to a later time. Alternatively, all apparently similar religious communities and needs are sometimes "lumped" together without proper differentiation. The problems that arise from this can be further aggravated by a tendency to view all Asians as Muslims and therefore to assume that, by meeting the needs of Muslims, the needs of all other religious communities of predominantly South Asian origin and composition will have been met.

Neither strategy was seen as effectively addressing religious needs or "mainstreaming" them. On several occasions, interviewees from demographically smaller groups described their communities as "minorities within minorities" and explained that, as a consequence, they felt powerless to make their demands heard or to have their needs met.

An example of this kind of failure was reported in relation to a last minute effort to organise a multi-faith ceremony to inaugurate a new political institution. It was decided that, as well as Christian representation, there would be a reading by a member of the Jewish tradition. When an enquiry was made as to whether a member of the Bahá'í community could also do a reading, she was told that other religions were invited to attend as "honoured guests", and that Bahá'ís would be represented by the Jewish participant. A Christian representative included in this event pointed out that a rushed and uninformed effort can end up causing more harm than good.

Some groups may also feel that their exclusion is deliberate, and not an oversight. A Unificationist who had been to many training seminars in both education and employment contexts stated that:

> ...what equality people talk about is a sham because they intimate that we're meant to respect all people except Moonies or Jehovah's Witnesses – it's almost like we can't escape.

Finding solutions

The two main suggestions made by respondents to the questionnaire survey were public education and improved awareness, and changes in the law. Other ideas included more flexibility and acceptance of religion, improving dialogue and acceptance between religious groups, improving multi-faith facilities, monitoring, and improving media representation.

At both local and national levels, a range of organisations and groups exist that aim to develop a positive awareness of religious diversity; to address tensions and conflicts between religions; and to facilitate dialogue between them. Such initiatives were generally welcomed both by interviewees from among the religious traditions and communities, and also by those from wider bodies and agencies. However, a number of interviewees expressed some concern about what they perceived to be the exclusivity of some of these initiatives, as a result of their focus on what are often perceived as the "mainstream" religions to the exclusion of other religious minorities.

This concern was particularly related to the exclusion of Pagans and people from New Religious Movements from some local inter-faith groups. This was thought to be at the behest of some national inter-faith organisations. One interviewee expressed their concern that a particular inter-faith organisation:

.........*seems to be focusing on ancient religions and sidelining new/non-mainstream and often non-Christian groups...it's important that 'newer' and new age groups be brought within the interfaith umbrella to support it rather than be a rival group...There was a recent meeting sponsored by the government regarding inter-faith. It was a grand occasion. There was the question, 'have all groups been invited?'; the answer was 'no'.*

Due to the size and visibility of the Christian and Muslim communities, concerns were expressed that what are described as "inter-faith" initiatives can, for practical purposes, exclude the concerns and interests of other religions. An instance was cited in which a prayer room initially established for "multi-faith" shared usage had become the exclusive domain of Muslims, on the basis that its use by other groups would render it unfit for Muslim use.

12   Political and pressure groups

Respondents to the postal questionnaire were asked if their organisation or its members had experienced unfair treatment[5] from non-religious groups – for example from political, community or pressure groups. If so, they were asked to state what kind of groups were involved and if possible to provide a specific example.

- A minority of respondents from every religious tradition said their organisation and its members had experienced unfair treatment from non-religious groups. The proportions reporting unfairness were generally lower than for the equivalent question about unfair treatment from other religious groups.
- Over a third of Muslim organisations and around a quarter of Jewish and Hindu organisations reported unfair treatment from non religious groups, compared with 16 per cent of Christian organisations and lower proportions of Sikhs, Buddhists and Bahá'ís. 10 of the 22 NRM/Pagan organisations replying to this question said they had experienced unfair treatment and the proportion of inter-faith organisations was also relatively high (one in three).
- Most of the Muslim organisations that quoted specific types of group involved in the unfair treatment mentioned political parties, right wing/racist groups or pressure groups. Christian organisations were more likely to mention central or local government, followed by the general public and political parties. Most Jewish and inter-faith respondents mentioned right wing/racist groups.

Unfair treatment from non-religious groups: quotes from the postal survey

Buddhists: *"complaints about facility usage"*, *"opposition to Buddhist school"*

Christians: *"exclusion by pubs and clubs"*, *"ethnic minorities get favoured treatment"*, *"gay group tried to close meeting"*, *"physical abuse"*, *"sabotage of displays"*, *"vandalism of church"*.

Hindus: *"insulting holy scriptures"*, *"interrupting street preachers"*

---

5   As with the previous question on unfair treatment from other religious groups, this question invited a simple yes/no answer.

Inter-faith: *"damage to worship areas"*, *"BNP campaign against Sikh centre"*, *"damage to property"*, *"no help given"*

Jews: *"hate literature"*

Muslims: *"windows broken"*, *"public outcry on purchasing building"*, *"outright hate"*, *"parking car in front of door"*, *"Labour Party is anti-Muslim"*

NRMs/Pagans: *"unable to rent rooms for events"*, *"support of satanic abuse myths"*, *"disruption to services"*, *"attempts to close bookshop"*, *"demonstrations in front of church"*

Sikhs: *"no representation in parliament"*

The main suggestions made by respondents were the same as for tackling unfair treatment from other religious groups - public education and improved awareness, and changes in the law. Other ideas included: more consultation with religious groups, improved representation in the media, policy reviews to promote equal treatment, the implementation and monitoring of voluntary codes of practice, and greater flexibility and acceptance of religion.

Discrimination is difficult to prove. It can always be said that it was an individual's attitude rather than an inadequate or discriminatory policy; as a result, you can't get action taken. People are laughing in your face: discrimination is an experience, the experience of a slap in the face.
Comment from a group of Jains and Hindus

....it's not out and out discrimination; not as bad as what ethnic minorities experience, but there's a whole part of your life people don't care about.
Comment from a group of Bahá'ís

This chapter returns to the questions posed by the research objectives. Inevitably, it contains more comment and interpretation than the purely factual material in the previous chapters.

Review of chapters 3-10

Chapters 3 to 10 looked at individual areas of life in isolation. This section draws together the findings from these areas.

Who is most likely to experience unfair treatment?

- A consistently higher level of unfair treatment was reported by Muslim organisations than by most other religious groups, both in terms of the proportion of respondents indicating that some unfair treatment was experienced, and by the proportion indicating that these experiences were frequent rather than occasional. The majority of Muslim organisations reported that their members experienced unfair treatment in every aspect of education, employment, housing, law and order, and in all the local government services covered in the questionnaire.
- Sikh and Hindu organisations also reported a high level of unfair treatment and tended to highlight the same areas of concern as Muslim organisations.
- Christian organisations in the survey were generally much less likely to report unfair treatment than Muslims, Sikhs and Hindus, and nearly all the unfair treatment they reported was 'occasional' rather than frequent.

- However, black-led Christian organisations and those representing groups such as Mormons and Jehovah's Witnesses were much more likely to report unfair treatment in nearly all walks of life than organisations in the 'mainstream' traditions. In the local interviews, such groups often described overt hostility similar to that experienced by some of the non-Christian minorities.

- Jewish organisations, in common with other religions, reported unfair treatment by journalists and the coverage of their religion by the media. In education, they singled out the behaviour of school pupils and higher education students, and arrangements for collective worship. In employment, they were more concerned about the attitudes and behaviour of managers and colleagues than the policies and practices of organisations.

- Notwithstanding the problems that continue to be experienced by Muslims, Hindus, Sikhs and Jews, the local interviews suggest that some of the traditions with fewer adherents regret that they lack the degree of recognition given to these groups. They have a feeling of being constantly overlooked: 'minorities within minorities'. This view was expressed by Bahá'ís and Zoroastrians, for example.

- Pagans and people from the New Religious Movements, on the other hand, were more likely to complain of open hostility and discrimination, and of being labelled as 'child abusers' and 'cults'.

Who is responsible?

The survey results suggest that unfair treatment is much more likely to be experienced in some areas of life than others.

- Overall, for every religious tradition, questions about the media tended to attract claims of unfair treatment from more organisations than other areas of the postal questionnaire. It was also noticeable that relatively more organisations said the unfairness was 'frequent' as opposed to 'occasional'.

- However, it was clear from both the survey and the local interviews that employment and education are also important areas of concern to every tradition. Most interviewees talked at greater length about these areas, and respondents to the survey indicated more unfair treatment, than was the case for services such as health, housing, transport and leisure.

- The religious traditions with a large membership of people from ethnic minorities (in particular Muslims, Sikhs and Hindus) were much more likely than other faith groups to report unfair treatment in areas such as immigration, policing and prisons.

The findings also suggest some tentative conclusions about the role played by the attitudes and behaviour of individuals compared with the policies and practices of organisations.

- In some areas of life (eg policing, prisons, immigration, health care, social services, transport) the attitudes and behaviour of staff employed by the service were seen by organisations from most religions as a more frequent source of unfair treatment than the policies of the organisations providing the service, although Muslim respondents, in particular, often felt that policies were at fault as well.
- In education and housing, pupils and neighbours or other tenants were often seen as the most likely source of unfair treatment. However, respondent organisations from some religions were equally likely to single out teachers.
- In employment, Christian and Jewish organisations were mainly concerned about the attitudes and behaviour of managers and colleagues, whereas other religions were also concerned about policy and practice.
- In the media, the attitudes and behaviour of journalists and presenters, and the coverage given to particular religions were both seen as relatively frequent sources of unfairness by respondents from all religions.

The policies and practices of employers and service providers can work (whether wittingly or unwittingly) to promote or reduce unfair treatment. Examples of policies that promote unfair treatment, as perceived by a number of research participants, would include arrangements for collective worship in schools, and immigration policy.

Policies to reduce discrimination will be of little use if the rhetoric is not translated into practice. Respondents to the survey recorded small but persistent differences between policy and practice, most noticeably in areas such as social services and policing, where practice attracted rather more claims of unfair treatment than policy. Muslim respondents were the most likely to indicate that practice was worse than policy. Interviewees representing employers and service providers gave some insights into the difficulties they were experiencing in translating policy into practice and often agreed that much remained to be done.

Finally, it could be claimed that the voluntary sector emerges slightly better in the views of respondents to the survey than either the public or private sectors. Management, staff, policies and practices of voluntary sector employers were all perceived as less unfair than their equivalents in the other sectors, as were the staff, policies and practices of registered social landlords compared with other housing providers. Charity staff responsible for funding were regarded as less unfair than their equivalents in central and local government, although views on policy and practice in this area were more mixed.

The nature and frequency of unfair treatment

Findings from the postal survey

Having covered education, employment, housing and so on, the questionnaire (see annex A) went on to ask some more general questions about the nature of unfair treatment and whether it was getting better or worse over time. Respondents were asked this time for their personal views, and requested to say how serious each problem was, rather than how frequent (whether problems had become more or less frequent over the last five years was asked in the next question). Because the following table gives percentages, only those religions with about 30 or more respondents for each question are included. Even so, the figures should be treated as very indicative.

Table 13.1   How serious do you think the following problems/experiences are for people within your religion?

	Very serious	Quite serious	Not at all serious	Don't know	Total responses (100%)
Ignorance					
Buddhist	9%	36%	39%	15%	33
Christian	18%	55%	22%	5%	285
Hindu	21%	58%	9%	12%	33
Jewish	17%	49%	34%	0%	35
Muslim	42%	44%	5%	9%	66
Sikh	22%	63%	9%	6%	32
Indifference					
Buddhist	3%	13%	68%	16%	31
Christian	20%	46%	29%	4%	282
Hindu	15%	58%	24%	3%	33
Jewish	9%	35%	53%	3%	34
Muslim	30%	45%	13%	12%	60
Sikh	13%	53%	25%	9%	32
Hostility					
Buddhist	6%	13%	71%	10%	31
Christian	6%	25%	62%	7%	279
Hindu	35%	35%	13%	16%	31
Jewish	12%	32%	53%	3%	34
Muslim	37%	47%	8%	8%	60
Sikh	25%	47%	19%	9%	32

Verbal abuse					
Buddhist	6%	13%	71%	10%	31
Christian	6%	23%	63%	9%	279
Hindu	27%	36%	21%	15%	33
Jewish	12%	47%	38%	3%	34
Muslim	35%	40%	13%	13%	63
Sikh	36%	48%	12%	3%	33
Physical abuse					
Buddhist	3%	13%	71%	13%	31
Christian	4%	8%	75%	12%	277
Hindu	28%	17%	31%	24%	29
Jewish	11%	25%	58%	6%	36
Muslim	28%	38%	16%	18%	61
Sikh	23%	52%	23%	3%	31
Damage to property					
Buddhist	3%	6%	81%	10%	31
Christian	7%	25%	57%	11%	283
Hindu	47%	25%	9%	19%	32
Jewish	11%	40%	43%	6%	35
Muslim	30%	36%	19%	16%	64
Sikh	33%	48%	12%	6%	33
Policies of organisations					
Buddhist	7%	17%	70%	7%	30
Christian	3%	20%	59%	19%	273
Hindu	7%	38%	24%	31%	29
Jewish	12%	15%	68%	6%	34
Muslim	16%	43%	16%	25%	63
Sikh	10%	32%	32%	26%	31
Practices of organisations					
Buddhist	6%	16%	68%	10%	31
Christian	4%	20%	56%	20%	271
Hindu	10%	42%	26%	23%	31
Jewish	12%	15%	71%	3%	34
Muslim	21%	43%	16%	21%	63
Sikh	14%	34%	28%	24%	29
Coverage in the media					
Buddhist	6%	34%	47%	13%	32
Christian	19%	39%	35%	7%	275
Hindu	32%	29%	19%	19%	31
Jewish	11%	28%	58%	3%	36
Muslim	48%	38%	5%	9%	66
Sikh	21%	36%	27%	15%	33

This table can be viewed in two ways: the issues or problems that appear to be of most concern to respondents from a particular religion, and the religious groups that are most likely to identify a particular problem.

Dealing first with the issues of most concern to particular religions:

- Only a minority of Muslim respondents said each issue was 'not at all serious', but media coverage, ignorance and hostility were the most likely to be identified as 'very serious'.
- In contrast, a clear majority of Buddhist respondents regarded most of the problems as 'not at all' serious, although there was more concern about ignorance and media coverage.
- The majority of Christian respondents were concerned to some degree about indifference, ignorance and media coverage (although more as a 'quite' serious problem than 'very serious') and very few identified physical abuse.
- Sikh and Hindu respondents, on the other hand, identified hostility, verbal and physical abuse and damage to property to a similar extent as Muslim respondents.
- Most Jewish respondents picked out ignorance, verbal abuse and damage to property, although mostly as a 'quite serious' problem.

Dealing with the religious groups that are most likely to identify particular problems/issues:

- Representatives from Muslim organisations were more likely than those from other religions to identify very serious problems in nearly every area.
- With the exception of Buddhists, a clear majority from every religion regarded ignorance as a very serious or quite serious problem.
- Media coverage and indifference were both regarded as very serious or quite serious by the majority of respondents from every type of religious organisation except Buddhist and Jewish.
- Muslims, Hindus and Sikhs were the most likely to identify hostility, verbal and physical abuse and damage to property as very or quite serious problems; Buddhists and Christians the least.
- Organisational policy and practice were generally less likely to be regarded as a serious problem, although more respondents indicated that they did not know the answer than for the other questions.

The issues most often identified as 'very serious' by the 23-25 representatives from NRM and Pagan groups who answered these questions were ignorance, hostility, verbal abuse and media coverage. For the 22-24 Bahá'í representatives it was ignorance, indifference and media coverage, mainly as 'quite serious'.

National and local organisations from within each religion highlighted broadly similar issues, but there were some variations. National Muslim organisations, for example, were more likely to identify ignorance and media coverage as 'very serious' than local Muslim organisations.

Are things getting better or worse?

Respondents were also asked for their personal views about whether, over the last five years, the kinds of problem listed above had become more frequent, less frequent, or stayed the same. As with the previous question, they could also tick 'don't know'. There was a fairly clear gradation in the views of people from different religions, ranging from those who thought things were generally getting worse through to those who detected improvements in every area.

Getting worse

- Muslim respondents were the most likely to think that problems had worsened. The majority thought that hostility, verbal abuse and unfair media coverage had all become more frequent. Views on indifference, and organisational policy and practice were fairly evenly divided. As far as the other problems were concerned, those who thought unfair treatment was becoming more frequent consistently outnumbered those who thought it was becoming less frequent, but they did not constitute a majority.
- Hindu respondents who thought that indifference, hostility and verbal abuse were more frequent exceeded those who thought these problems were now less frequent, but in general the views of Hindus were quite mixed.

Much the same

- Christian respondents were fairly evenly divided between those who thought ignorance, indifference and unfair media coverage had become more frequent and those who thought it had stayed the same. However, a clear majority thought that all the other problems had stayed the same. Anglicans and people from Independent Churches were more likely to say that ignorance, indifference and unfair media coverage were increasing than the other Christian denominations.
- Most Jewish respondents felt that the frequency of all these experiences had stayed the same. Those who detected change tended to think that verbal and physical abuse, damage to property and unfairness in organisational policy and practice had become less frequent rather than more.

Getting better
- Most of the answers given by Sikhs were fairly evenly divided between 'less frequent' and 'stayed the same', with a smaller number of respondents opting to say that problems had become more frequent.
- The majority of Buddhist and Bahá'í respondents thought that ignorance was now less frequent and that all the other problems had either stayed the same or become less frequent.
- The 21-23 respondents from inter-faith groups mostly indicated that problems had become 'less frequent' or 'stayed the same'.
- A clear majority of the 23-25 NRM/Pagan respondents thought that ignorance, indifference, hostility and unfair media coverage were now less frequent and that the other problems had either become less frequent or stayed the same.

National and local organisations within each religion took broadly similar views. However, there were a few disparities: for example, local Muslim organisations were more likely to say that problems with policy and practice were becoming less frequent, and national Muslim organisations to say that they were becoming more frequent.

Local interviews

Interviewees recorded a variety of views about the seriousness and frequency of religious discrimination. Especially for those who are members of the visible minorities or are members of New Religious Movements, overt expressions of discrimination can impact upon their lives in quite dramatic ways. For others, the perceived hurt may be more subtle, but still painful. For example, a group of Bahá'ís commented about their experience to the effect that:

> ....it's not out and out discrimination; not as bad as what ethnic minorities experience, but there's a whole part of your life people don't care about.

Older interviewees often indicated that, over the years, there had been a trend towards more tolerance and yet, paradoxically, this seemed to be coupled with greater ignorance. Some thought that harassment and hostility towards individuals had become less overt than previously. But the consequences of continued ignorance and lack of understanding could ultimately be more serious and far-reaching since these can be embodied in institutionalised manifestations of discrimination. Having survived the overt hostility, the grounds of struggle were now moving to demands for equality, which had more far-reaching implications.

A Roman Catholic noted that:

> *We only want parity, not preferential treatment.... in a western society in the 21st century this is not too much to ask.*

Interviewees across all religions and the secular agencies noted a variety of negative attitudes. These arose mainly from the general public's ignorance of other than Christian religions, and the seeming inability of people to understand religious differences and/or the commonalities between religions.

Ignorance

In the local interviews, ignorance was one of the most frequently cited reasons for unfair or discriminatory treatment on the basis of religion. Despite living side by side, sometimes for decades or even hundreds of years, a large number of interviewees from minority religions and communities felt that the rest of society know very little about them. For example, one individual explained that a neighbour was *"shocked"* to find out that Jews don't celebrate Christmas/Jesus. A Zoroastrian youth reported that when other young people ask about her religion, they often ask if she attends church. She tells them her temple is in London and they reply that *"it can't be a real religion if you only have one temple"*.

A member of the Church of Jesus Christ of Latter-day Saints highlighted the ignorance that people often have about movements such as this, and which is reinforced by a relative lack of reliable public information. This member reported that the local library has refused to carry any literature about their Church:

> *So if you go to the library, you won't find anything other than the Book of Mormon in comparison to stacks of information on Hindus, Muslims, etc....So instead of people finding out about the Church through a library or by coming to the church, they believe what the media present or word of mouth. So much happens out of ignorance, but people won't take the trouble to find out. This is exacerbated by negative messages coming from schools, Christian church, possibly the government.*

A female Muslim youth worker described an experience in which halal meat was cooked on a separate barbeque, and yet then was put on the same plate as other meat and so the Muslim students present could not eat it.

Ignorant attitudes towards people of different religions may also take the form of nasty comments made by local residents as families go to their place of worship, or in comments like, *"what's wrong with your head"*, as one Sikh man used to be asked. Remarks like, *"where's the fancy dress?"*, as reported by a Muslim woman, are also not uncommon.

Often people who were the recipients of offensive comments found it hard to know whether the ignorance and lack of common sense that was demonstrated came from a lack of interest or from a deep-seated hostility. One youth felt that most people seemed unable to understand needs which ultimately were not all that different from their own. He described them as having *"a brick in front of their eyes"* – literally a mental block.

Fear and suspicion

Interviewees often reported considerable levels of fear and suspicion towards people who have a strong religious identity and commitment. It was noted that, especially if others have had a bad experience of religion or of religious people, they tend to generalise this to all other members of that particular religious group, or even to all religions. One person felt that there is a section of the general public which believes that that people who maintain strong religious beliefs and distinctive practices are:

> *...dangerous, clinging to old, outmoded ways, clinging to their identity – people don't understand and are suspicious of those who don't want to conform, who want to keep their distinct identity and not completely integrate.*

These tendencies are further compounded by the fact that even when members of the public are not ill-disposed towards religious groups, there can be a tendency to treat religion as something of a "taboo" subject in normal social discourse. Many people seem afraid to ask about others' religions for fear of giving offence.

At the same time, from within the religious communities, there was recognition of a need to get beyond a *"siege mentality"*. Many felt that the biggest problems arise when people feel insecure, especially around issues of Welsh and English national identity. As a result, they resist any diversity issue. One Bahá'í noted that her religion is very much a world religion and one of its central concerns is to do with being a world citizen. But she observed that:

> *Just because you have something that goes beyond nationality doesn't mean you don't love your country.*

A number of interviewees noted that the most recent newcomers to local areas often bear the brunt of negative attitudes. This issue was raised in a number of contexts where references were made to concerns about newcomers or people from "different" communities constituting a "threat" to the well-being of more established local communities. This was especially felt to be the case in areas that already suffered significant deprivation, disenfranchisement and polarisation.

Preconceptions, negative stereotypes and misconceptions

Preconceptions may not always be negative, but can be misleading. A Jewish man was told:

> Oh, you're Jewish! You must have a wonderful family life.

One man described how women used to be teased when wearing trousers and skirts together, but that now it's "the fashion". He felt, however, that this is not because this is seen to be of equal cultural value, but because the dominant culture wants "to include those bits within its own – not to value them". A woman recalled that she had read about a designer who incorporated the head scarf into his designs:

> First of all, it was so hypocritical when socially and politically, Muslim people and Muslim women are so excluded and devalued. But second, the scarf was matched with a shorter skirt which ultimately is offensive as it was a religious thing, but its match with something that went against practices was bizarre.

A support professional recalled being told "I've never met a Pakistani woman like you before". She explained that she wondered if she is considered outspoken because she has "a big mouth" or because she contradicts the stereotype. Another woman reported that she does not usually wear a headscarf except for major holidays and that:

> People usually smile at me, but when I wear it [a head scarf] it seems that they don't want to know you; they think you're thick...if you wear a head scarf people assume you don't speak English.

Another woman concurred, explaining that:

> When people see a Muslim woman in full dress they just assume she's pregnant, uneducated, illiterate.

One woman reported an instance in which a local health club refused to allow Asian female members because it thought that this would "put off" other customers. The same club did employ Asian women staff, but only those who wore western dress.

A Sikh noted that people think because someone is wearing a kirpan, then he is aggressive or dangerous. A Jehovah's Witness observed that people believe that they are "*uneducated and brainwashed*" and spoke of a public perception of Jehovah's Witnesses being involved in a "*controlling American organisation*" despite the fact that a central part of their beliefs is focused on actively developing and following their own conscience.

Social stigma and "being awkward"

Many interviewees reported feeling that social stigma and perceptions of anti-social behaviour were associated with difference, particularly around the need to abstain from common social practices on the grounds of religious convictions and traditions. This was a concern particularly for Bahá'ís, Jehovah's Witnesses, Muslims and Quakers.

One religiously observant individual recalled how, some time ago, his children did not like to go shopping with him and his wife because they always read the labels due to their very strict diet. The children were embarrassed because the shopkeepers would always seem to look suspiciously at his parents because of their doing this. However, he noted the irony that "*now everyone reads labels!*". Another woman remarked with regard to food that:

> ... you're already different – your colour, your dress – and now you're asking what's in things, but if you don't know, you have to ask.

A number of interviewees felt that others assumed that, in following their religious beliefs and practices, they were just "*being awkward*" or were troublemakers. Yet such interviewees are themselves often overcome with feelings of awkwardness as they try to find ways to "*to fit in*" or "*try not to be difficult*" (by, for example, participating in common activities like having lunch with colleagues at pubs) whilst still maintaining the requirements of their religions. One woman reported that she found this especially hard because she is always concerned that if she raises a problem, then people will say: "*you know, we try to treat them like everyone else and they don't want that*".

This woman observed that people such as her do not want to be seen as different, but they would like to have an environment that is appropriate, sensitive and acceptable to their religious needs, so that they do not constantly have to experience these tensions.

Discussion

This section returns to a couple of questions that were raised by the research objectives: the extent to which religious discrimination is real or perceived, and the extent to which it overlaps with racial discrimination.

Real or perceived – and is it discrimination?

Unfair treatment does not have to be deliberate, or even detected by the victim, to constitute discrimination. On the other hand, even a deliberate act which is perceived by others as unfair does not necessarily constitute discrimination. This section deals with some of the problems raised by research participants by analogy with what might be concluded if the same allegation were made of unfair treatment on the basis of gender, race or disability.

A group of Hindus and Jains who were interviewed explained the difficulty and anguish that suspicion of their reported experience can cause for those who seek to articulate it to a wider audience. As they expressed this, such a response can compound the pain of the original experience.

> *Discrimination is difficult to prove. It can always be said that it was an individual's attitude rather than an inadequate or discriminatory policy; as a result, you can't get action taken. People are laughing in your face: discrimination is an experience, the experience of a slap in the face.*

The status of violence, verbal abuse and criminal damage as forms of 'unfair treatment' and discriminatory behaviour cannot be in any doubt. The postal survey suggested they were very real concerns for those representing Muslims, Sikhs and Hindus. Fear of violence did not seem to be a widespread issue in the local interviews, but examples were given, for example, of criminal damage.

Participants in the research quoted other examples of unfair treatment (for example in employment practices) which would be unlawful if practised on grounds of race, gender or disability, or which might be in contravention of the Human Rights Act. In the postal survey, organisations representing visible minorities, particularly Muslims, frequently identified problems with organisational policy or practice as well as with the attitudes and behaviour of individuals.

Ignorance and indifference towards religion were of widespread concern to research participants, irrespective of whether they came from 'minority' or 'majority' religions. This theme came up many times in the local interviews and was echoed in the postal survey. In some cases this reflected a sense of hurt that the wider society did not seem to care about strongly held beliefs, or even to show the slightest interest or curiosity. People from all traditions expressed regret about the lack of recognition and respect for religion and for the role it played in their lives. For people from minority religions, there was the additional problem that lack of knowledge inevitably causes offence sooner or later, even if unintentional, and especially if there appears to be no will to understand.

Ignorance and indifference do not in themselves constitute discrimination, although it was clear from examples given by interviewees that they cause much pain on a person to person basis. However, in organisational settings they can contribute to an environment in which discrimination of all kinds (including 'unwitting' and institutional discrimination) is able to thrive. Although lack of interest or curiosity sound like one of the mildest possible forms of unfair treatment, the context is important. They could be harmful in a teacher, police officer or planner, for example. In other contexts, however, religious individuals can come close to claiming that others are discriminating against them because they do not happen to share the same values.

Giving offence can work in both directions. Research participants, including those representing secular agencies, spoke often of the offence caused by the reactions of the wider society to the beliefs and practices of some religions. There was perhaps rather less recognition of the offence that may be caused to others in society by the nature of some religious beliefs and practices. However, strength of belief and the degree to which a religion seeks converts were acknowledged by some interviewees as factors which may influence the response of others (*"the more active you are, the more vulnerable you become"*).

Representatives from certain traditions were also concerned that their very existence went unrecognised, either because so little was known or taught about them or because they were being deliberately excluded. Such groups felt like 'minorities within minorities' who were being ignored by schools, employers, policy makers and service providers, even though these institutions may be working hard to include and involve the 'majority-minority' religions. Some people attributed this exclusion to the size and visibility of numerically more powerful religions. However, some of the groups that are excluded in this way may also be regarded as too controversial or challenging.

Although religious beliefs and secular law can sometimes be at odds with one another, specific conflicts between religious requirements and those of the law did not often emerge as a theme in the local interviews. There were, however, a few instances (see, for example, the chapter on health care).

The other way in which some religious groups may view the law as itself discriminatory is in the Establishment of the Church of England and in the existence of statutes such as the Act of Settlement. Again, however, these two issues were rarely raised as everyday concerns. The inequity of the present legal position in the common law on blasphemy attracted rather more comment, but opinions were divided as to how this issue should be addressed.

Some of the other issues of which research participants complained are problems that are widely shared by the rest of society: for example, the view that the media never presents positive news stories, or complaints about the scheduling of programmes on television.

Is discrimination based on religion or on race and ethnicity?
Many of the people quoted in this report have referred to their appearance when describing some aspect of religious discrimination. This raises the question as to whether the experiences they describe are really a reaction by other people to their race or culture. In some cases research participants referred to items of dress or diet that they would see as religious requirements. Some argue that hostility shown to white converts who adopt the forms of dress and other practices of their new religion is proof of discrimination based on religion; others that perpetrators motivated by racism associate these outward signs with ethnic minority groups.

It was beyond the scope of this research to find out whether those responsible for hostility, abuse or overt discrimination interpret such signals in a religious or racial sense. However, it is noticeable that black-led Christian organisations were consistently more likely to report unfair treatment than other Christian organisations, that religions with large numbers of visible minorities (Sikhs, Hindus, Muslims) recorded the most unfair treatment overall, and that comments made in response to the postal survey and in interviews frequently referred to unfair treatment as a form of racism.

On the other hand there were clearly some claims of unfair treatment – for example, made by white people of British descent with no outward, visible signs of their religion – which, if valid, cannot be attributed to anything other than religion or belief. Pagans and members of New Religious Movements, in particular, reported a degree of hostility which often seemed to match the experiences of visible minorities, and they also drew attention to stereotyping and sensationalism in the media.

This suggests that whilst some discrimination is purely racial, and some purely religious, there is an area of overlap where those responsible for discrimination and those who experience it might both have difficulty coming down on the side of one 'explanation' or the other. Chapter 2 indicated the extent to which many religious organisations acknowledged the existence of such an overlap.

It was pointed out in one interview that whilst many religious people regard religion as an intrinsic part of their identity, the rest of society tends to think of it as optional. Religiously observant individuals discover that their strongly held beliefs and religious requirements are treated by others as if they were negotiable. This is something that could not be expected in respect of race and would not generally be regarded as acceptable in respect of ethnicity.

Some interviewees felt that attempts to draw a rigid and artificial distinction – for example between religion and culture – could in themselves lead to unfair treatment. An example was given in relation to local authority funding arrangements, where religious groups sometimes had to present or reinvent themselves as cultural groups in order to obtain funding for the services they provide. At the same time, some people from religions that are not associated with ethnic minority groups felt that such groups receive more favourable treatment from local authorities because they are able to take advantage of equal opportunity and diversity policies from which their own organisations are excluded.

You need to make people aware, to have access to information, but you also need a way of making such things not optional – establishing these as responsibilities is key; that's possibly where law comes in.

Comment from an interviewee

This chapter describes the views of interviewees and respondents to the postal survey and does not offer any comment on the different solutions that are proposed. However, as mentioned in chapter 1, the Home Office has commissioned a separate study which looks at the legal options in more detail.

Findings from the postal survey

The people completing questionnaires on behalf of religious organisations were asked for their personal views about the measures that should be considered in order to combat unfair treatment. Each respondent was asked to tick up to three items from a list of six (to which they could also add their own suggestions) or to indicate that they did not think any new measures were necessary.

In practice, some people ticked up to six measures from the list and the average number varied between religious groups. This means that comparisons between traditions need to be treated with caution: where organisations from a particular religion ticked 4 or 5 options, percentages based on the number of respondents favouring an option will look high in comparison with other traditions, whilst percentages based on the number of responses will look low. In order to avoid this, the summary below concentrates on the two or three options most likely to be chosen by respondents from within each tradition. The full results are given in annex C (part 3).

- More teaching of comparative religion in schools was the first or second most favoured option for all the non-Christian traditions, and for representatives of organisations in the Christian (other) category.
- Public education programmes and better training of staff/employees were the two most popular options for Christian respondents. Both these measures (especially public education) were also well favoured by respondents from the other religions.

- The remaining three measures (changes in the law, policy reviews to promote equal treatment and voluntary codes of practice) were less popular. However, changes in the law was the single most popular option for Muslims (chosen by slightly more respondents than comparative religion). It was the least favoured measure for Christian respondents, although within this tradition it had more support from representatives of black-led organisations.
- Sikh respondents were more likely than respondents from other religions to favour policy reviews, although they gave higher priority to comparative religion overall.
- Voluntary codes of practice was one of the least favoured options for all religions.
- Only a tiny minority favoured no new action (six per cent of Christian respondents and smaller percentages for the other religions).
- National and local organisations within most religions took a broadly similar view. However, local Muslim organisations placed more emphasis on comparative religion and less on changes in the law or on public education programmes than did national Muslim organisations.

A number of the written-in suggestions centred around the need for different faiths to work together, and the need for a change in attitude by the media, possibly backed up by some form of watchdog.

Local interviews

Changing demographics and identities
Interviewees both from religious traditions and secular agencies noted the significant demographic changes that have taken place in England and Wales in recent years. These changes have brought challenges for the inherited sense of national identity in both countries and have underlined the need to accommodate a more diverse range of identities. Religion has a role and significance in individual and community identity that might contribute to this process.

Interviewees in England, especially, acknowledged a sincerity and reality about the developing pluralism. But it was felt that the apparent diversity does not always go that deep. A Zoroastrian illustrated this by explaining that he can share a meal with Muslims and speak Urdu; can have tea with Hindus and speak Gujarati; and can go to a Rotary Club function, speak English and eat with all six knives and forks. People then say that he has "*made it*". But he then went on to ask:

If this is 'making it', then why are my own children expected to only eat fish and chips?

An advice worker remarked that:

...true cosmopolitanism is where diversity is reproduced in everything, everything you do, see, where you go: it's as if we still have black and white doors: the signs are no longer there, but there are definitely places I wouldn't go.

In Wales, because of the historical struggle to maintain and assert Welsh identity and language over and against English assimilationism, there is an additional layer of complexity in these issues. Perhaps as a consequence, a number of interviewees felt that urban areas in Wales were still about twenty to thirty years behind those in England in dealing with broader diversities issues. In rural areas, the situation was felt to be a further ten years behind.

A number of interviewees pointed out that, unlike in England, in Wales there had not, as yet, been the major social conflicts (such as the urban disturbances of the early 1980s) to underline how bad things were. This had led to a dangerous complacency:

There was no riot in Cardiff in the 1980's, so no one bothered. No one was rewarded for their good behaviour. In the absence of riots, there were no initiatives to come about, like Scarman.

The newly devolved level of government in Wales was seen to provide a context in which it might be possible to avoid former mistakes and to address existing inequities. However, it was also noted that, so far, comparatively little attention had been given to issues of religious identity, inclusiveness and discrimination compared with the degree to which race, gender and disability had succeeded in getting onto the agenda of devolved government in Wales.

Paying attention and acting

During the course of the local research, a significant number of individuals, organisational representatives, and community groups expressed concerns both about the basis upon which they were being asked to participate and about what might or might not be done with the results. A youth worker noted that, in general, the biggest complaint of young people is that they are not included in dialogue about the issues that affect them. But another emphasised that:

...before you even ask young people what they think, you have to have people in policy/government positions who are able to understand and act effectively; which you don't currently have. This really raises their hopes, when the government isn't even in a position to do anything; this could be harmful.

In considering the legal and other options for tackling unfair treatment on the basis of religion, the message of the local interviews is that those affected by these problems are not just sitting back and waiting for external agencies and/or measures to change things. Rather, they are developing their own empowerment from "inside" and "below". Policies and laws from "outside" and from "above" are seen as instruments that can either impede or facilitate change. They can be imposed upon those primarily affected by the problems concerned, or they can be developed in partnership with them. They can create more divisions and difficulties, or they can help to move things along in a more positive and inclusive direction.

Co-operative and complementary approaches

The local interviews suggest that a complementary approach based on measures from "within" communities and measures from "outside" will be necessary. A number of people gave voice to the kinds of challenge involved:

Without co-operation, no law will help...

There is a wide gap between policy and practice...It is due to inner prejudice which is difficult to address. People I've worked with have become so close that they forget I'm from the Muslim community when they launch into criticisms. It takes a generation for attitudes to change. It has taken years of working together with the people around us, giving them access to, and understanding of, my culture, my family. Only then will they treat me at their level. Only then is there an element of trust.

...people who are oppressors, it is not a matter of more information. The only thing to change is their own will to change. Ultimately it is a process of personal development for each individual.

There was a considerable consensus among individuals, organisations and groups from within the religious traditions that a more inclusive policy approach is needed. This would be an approach that at all levels and sectors of society promotes a recognition of the distinctiveness of religious identity and its relationship with other key dimensions of personal and social life.

The law

Interviewees often commented on the usefulness or otherwise of existing laws against racial discrimination and on the possibilities and pitfalls of using the law to prohibit religious discrimination. There were divergent views about the detailed ways in which the law might be used, but significant numbers felt that, in concert with other measures, it had a part to play in terms of setting standards and expectations as well as in being a means of enforcement and remedy where discrimination is deliberate or where change and accommodation might not otherwise occur.

Existing law: problems and possibilities

Race Relations Act 1976

Interviewees expressed views both for and against extending the Race Relations Act to include discrimination on the basis of religion. Some people drew attention to inconsistencies in the existing legislation.

> I can't see how religion couldn't be part of the Race Relations Act: if someone is using something about you to highlight your difference to other people, to harm you, I don't see how you could separate religion out of the RRA. You end up saying that if someone says 'black bastard', they're racist, but if they make a slur about someone's religion, they're simply 'ignorant'.

It was also pointed out that, because of case law, the Act did already cover some groups (eg Sikhs) that can be defined in terms of religion as well race or ethnicity. The exclusion of other religious groups (eg Muslims) was felt by some in the groups not covered to be, in itself, an expression of unfair treatment on the basis of religion.

It was also noted that the fact that the Act does not currently prohibit religious discrimination sometimes has a distorting effect on the way in which religious groups have had to present themselves, and on the development of appropriate service provision to meet the needs of such groups. As a white, female, policy officer put it:

> People have had to try to fit religion into a racial mould. Muslims, for example, are not covered, yet the issue is about religion. If we just followed the Race Relations Act, and just did the minimum, our services would be very poor.

An alternative view, expressed by a number of interviewees, was that religious discrimination needed to be addressed in its own terms. Trying to append religion to race might result in the specificity of both agendas being dissipated. In the words of an African-Caribbean/Asian of Trinidadian family background:

> I would not like to see religion appended to existing legislation; even race issues become appended to things and get lost and clouded; it should not be seen as part of a package, although there are interrelations as it's another block to being able to see a person for who they are.

Crime and Disorder Act 1998

A white, male, member of a mediation organisation believed that the Crime and Disorder Act could be utilised to mediate between victims and perpetrators of religious abuse, arguing that:

> The Crime and Disorder Act has within it an incredible opportunity to practice restorative justice.

Another interviewee who supports the victims of racial harassment noted that this Act, whilst creating offences covering racially aggravated harassment, failed to do the same for offences involving religious hostility. A number of interviewees expressed the view that this was a missed opportunity. The support worker quoted above felt that an holistic view of harassment might be useful to victims and that religious discrimination/harassment could, as a specific dimension of anti-social behaviour, be brought within the purview of the Crime and Disorder Act. Others, however, thought it would be difficult to distinguish between racial and religious incidents. A white, male, police inspector noted that:

> ...an incident may start as a road rage incident and then move to racial insults, even if it wasn't initially motivated by race. There's the same problem with religion: it might begin as racial harassment but then elements of religion are brought into it.

The Human Rights Act

The Human Rights Act came into force soon after the research was completed and awareness of this Act was not, perhaps, as widespread as one might have expected among interviewees from religious traditions, communities and organisations. A number who were aware of it, however, expressed concerns about how it might be implemented. A white, female, legal adviser also expressed uncertainty about the impact of Article 14 of the European Convention on Human Rights, which prohibits discrimination on the basis of, amongst other grounds, race or religion, since:

It is unclear how it will be enforced or manifested in policy, especially because you have to breach another aspect of law in terms of discrimination for it to be enforceable.

Nevertheless, a number of people drew attention to what one Asian male interviewee called the *"massive implications"* that they believe the Act will have – not only in terms of protection but also in setting out responsibilities and obligations with regard to religious groups within a plural society. One interviewee said of the Act that it will at least *"provide rights to individuals regardless of who they are"*.

The Christian "default position"

Interviewees from secular agencies as well as religious groups pointed out that there was a Christian 'default position' built into some existing laws. Many felt that this amounted to unfair treatment of other religions and should be reviewed, although what might take the place of the default position was the subject of much more diverse comment.

Blasphemy

A few interviewees from within religious traditions referred to the common law offences of blasphemy. Some felt that these provisions, if reformed so to apply more widely than to Christianity alone, would signal the need to respect individuals and communities of diverse religious belief and provide a legal remedy for the more defamatory kinds of unfair treatment on the basis of religion. As one interviewee put it:

...freedom of speech doesn't include the right to inflame [or to] impinge on the rights of others.

Others, however, expressed caution about this and argued that it would be better to abolish the existing blasphemy offences – since they were currently a symbol of religious exclusivity, offering privileged protection to Christianity alone – and replace them with measures preventing incitement to religious hatred.

The Act of Settlement

Some Christian interviewees raised aspects of constitutional law that embody unfair treatment on the basis of religion. A Roman Catholic drew attention to the fact that, under the law, Roman Catholic Christians are still the only religious group to which a direct successor to the Throne is not allowed to belong. This interviewee believed that these legal constraints remained in force because of persistent perceptions and myths about Catholic disloyalty.

He felt that such things would be considered an outrage if they were in force in respect, say, of black people, and argued that a failure to alter this legal position helped to perpetuate the myths. He noted that the Government had challenged the hereditary principle in relation to the composition of the House of Lords and he could not therefore see why the Act of Settlement should not be repealed. He acknowledged, however, that "establishment" in general, including royalty, still held an appeal for many religious communities and individuals, as well as for those in positions of authority.

Potential new law: problems and possibilities

A substantial number of interviewees saw a role for the law in tackling unfair treatment on the basis of religion. This did not necessarily mean a law on religious discrimination as such, although this was advocated by a number of interviewees. A wide variety of views were expressed on this by those representing both religious communities and secular agencies. For example, as a Hindu expressed it:

> *At national level, the government is duty bound, through enactment of laws, to protect people from discrimination based on their religion.*

Such interviewees felt that law was an important dimension in the social legitimation and recognition of any issue; that it could create a sense of obligation; and that it could lead to the development of a wider supportive infrastructure that would help individuals and groups challenge discrimination on the basis of religion.

A number of other interviewees felt that the need for a specific legal measure or measures in relation to religious discrimination was not established or justified. A representative of an employment tribunal was concerned that it would be difficult to define religion and to determine whether someone is a "true" believer. He concluded that there is:

> *...absolutely no cause/need for religious discrimination law [since] case law has sorted out these problems.*

Some interviewees were also concerned that any attempt to define religion and enshrine freedom from religious discrimination in English law might not be in the best interests of their own religions. As a member of the Church of the Latter-day Saints put it:

> *...what will be acceptable and what won't? No matter how well you write that law, it's subject to different interpretations. Politicians would challenge and amend the law, and would end up with a law that is completely opposite to what faith communities presented in the first place.*

Some concerns were expressed that a law on religious discrimination might also be subject to misuse. Others felt that whilst religious discrimination should not be tolerated, religion should not be enshrined as a separate ground on the basis that this could be dangerous and contribute to further tensions, prompting divisions between religious communities and a backlash from the wider society. One interviewee felt that making a special case for individual adherents of religious beliefs might:

> *...get peoples' hackles up; why should they get special attention?*

Another argued that using the law as a "stick" to bring about change was *"not the way"*, because it:

> *...alienates the communities you're seeking to provide for AND creates backlash/hostilities from the host community ...*

Drawing attention to what she thought was a tendency for some religions to be more dominant and dominating than others, one interviewee said that by enacting a specific law on religious discrimination:

> *...you give extra license to those religions, you are asking for trouble, and possibly creating a divisive society. There needs to be room for discretion, through raising awareness.*

New generic equalities Laws

Partly because of this concern about isolating religion and treating it as a special ground a number of interviewees from both religious communities and secular agencies preferred an approach based on cultural diversity. This was thought to hold fewer dangers than singling out religion in a way that might actually foster communalism through the legal entrenchment of religious differences.

Two models emerged here. One approach, that was advocated by a youth worker and was previously noted in chapter 2, argued for looking at both religious discrimination and racial discrimination within a broader context of "cultural discrimination":

> *...if you use the term 'cultural discrimination', and look more holistically at the issues, you can begin to approach the issue in terms of 'whether the communities' needs and cultural aspirations are being met' rather than trying to determine whether racial or religious discrimination or determining what discrimination is, and categorising the problems people have...*

Another, even more generic approach, was to tackle religious discrimination through fully integrated legislation on equalities, rather than use separate religious, ethnic and gender-based protections. Those supporting this view advocated the creation of an inclusive *Equalities Act* of a kind that could encompass legal protection for communities as well as individuals.

Intelligent legislation

Whilst a wide variety of views were expressed during the local interviews, there was a general scepticism about reliance on the law. Partly, this was because people felt that the law has had a relatively ineffective track record in terms of enforcement in other contexts such as racial discrimination. For example, several members of a youth group did not favour extending or amending the *Race Relations Act* because:

> ...laws are always made to be broken; [much] depends on how it is implemented and it is rarely implemented properly. [There is] still racism, still inequality etc. despite all the laws.

Another interviewee commented with reference to existing racial discrimination law:

> ...the Race Relations Act is not only not strong or effective enough to provide needed protection, but cases drag on.

Most interviewees therefore felt it inappropriate, unwise, or ineffective to rely on law alone. But there was strong support for holistic and comprehensive approaches that could learn the lessons of the limitations experienced in race equality law and policy, and the use of law in combination with other strategies was often advocated:

> ...as with race relations, we've seen that law can't remove prejudices, but we have seen walls breaking down, and after 30 years, there is a better climate.

Many pointed to the need for a context to legislation in which awareness is raised and information disseminated, on the basis of which a sense of responsibility can be engendered and developed:

> You need to make people aware, to have access to information, but you also need a way of making such things not optional – establishing these as responsibilities is key; that's possibly where law comes in.

This suggests a desire for what might be called "intelligent legislation". This approach recognises the potential effectiveness of the law in particular areas. It can provide an important social and political message about religious inclusivity and the unacceptability of discrimination. As one interviewee put it, people need *"the stick that law provides."* To be "intelligent legislation" that contributes to wider positive social change it was generally felt important that any legal measures needed to be combined with effective guidance, good practice, and support for implementation. An advice worker noted that the imposition of obligations without an effective system of monitoring would be ineffective as a means of dealing with religious discrimination:

...once you establish an obligation, you need to establish a way of following up by providing resources and guidance.

Another interviewee argued that to bring about change as well as to provide remedies:

You need reporting, bench-marking data, peer group pressure.

Conclusion

Participants in the research favoured a holistic approach in which education, training, and a bigger effort to teach more about comparative religion in schools were all recommended. This is in line with repeatedly expressed views about the role of ignorance in fostering religious discrimination by both individuals and organisations, and with the view expressed in interviews that the media were one of the main barriers to change.

There was scepticism about voluntary codes of practice, but also realism about the law. Some changes might be needed in order to *"send the right messages about discrimination"* but law on its own would not suffice. It was not a panacea, but could help if used judiciously and in conjunction with other approaches. Changes in the law were most supported by people from ethnic minority groups, many of whom will have had experience of its strengths and limitations from the existing legislation on racial discrimination.

In face to face interviews, it was pointed out that the changes needed from employers and service providers were not necessarily expensive: quite small adaptations could be very helpful and sometimes it was as simple as trying to ensure that people weren't made to feel awkward. There was a role for better guidelines and *"worked examples"*. It was felt that employers and educationalists, in particular, could do more to accommodate religious diversity, and in a less grudging way.

In areas such as planning and funding, more 'mainstreaming' was required and greater acknowledgement of the services that religious organisations provide to their own – and sometimes the wider – community.

Those from the less well known and the less 'mainstream' religions stressed the need for more inclusiveness – for example when holding events or carrying out consultation exercises.

Some interviewees, young as well as old, described a process of change and improvement to which they themselves had contributed. They suggested that religious communities could take some of the initiative themselves.

The project findings offer an evidence base in support of the conclusion of the Interim Report, published in January 2000, that it is 'unlikely given the multifaceted nature and dimensions of unfair treatment on the basis of religion that any single response would be adequate or effective.' The one previously identified option that the findings of the present report indicate would not be adequate to the described experience of unfair treatment and discrimination would be that of no new response. The Interim Report, which includes examples of possible policy options, is available on www.multifaithnet.org/projects/religdiscrim/reports.htm).

RELIGIOUS DISCRIMINATION IN ENGLAND AND WALES

QUESTIONNAIRE

This questionnaire offers your organisation an opportunity to take part in a survey on religious discrimination. The survey forms part of a research project that has been commissioned by the Home Office. More details about the research are given in the enclosed leaflet or at the project website (www.multifaithnet.org). Organisations responding to this questionnaire will not be identified by name in any report arising from the project.

If you have any queries, please contact:
the Project Secretaries:
Michele Wolfe (e-mail M.M.Wolfe@derby.ac.uk)
Sima Parmar (e-mail S.Parmar@derby.ac.uk)
Tel 01332 592088

Please return the completed questionnaire in the FREEPOST envelope provided by **March 24th 2000**.

Religious Discrimination Research Project
Religious Resource and Research Centre
FREEPOST DY869
University of Derby
Mickleover
DERBY DE3 5GX

Thank you very much for your participation.

CODE	
	1
	2
	3

SECTION A: YOUR ORGANISATION

First of all, we would like to ask you some details about your organisation.

1. Which of the following best describes the religion of your organisation?
   (Please tick one box. If your organisation particularly identifies with a denomination or
   "movement" please write this in alongside.)

   Name of denomination or movement [5]

Bahá'í	1	
Buddhist	2	
Christian	3	
Hindu	4	
Jain	5	
Jewish	6	
Muslim	7	
Pagan	8	
Rastafarian	9	
Sikh	10	
Zoroastrian	11	
Inter-Faith (please describe)	12	
Other (please specify)	13	

2. Which of the following best describes the scope of your organisation's work?
   (please tick as many boxes as apply)

Local	1
Regional	2
National	3
International	4

3. Do the activities of your organisation cover mostly urban or rural areas?
   (please tick appropriate box)

Urban	1
Rural	2
Both urban and rural	3

4. In which local authority area is your organisation located? (please give the name of the local
   authority district or borough)

5. Under a) please tick up to **three** boxes which best describe the **main** activities of your organisation.

   Under b) please tick any boxes which describe other activities of your organisation.

	9-11	12-25		
	a) Main activities (please tick up to 3)	**b) Other activities** (please tick as many as apply)		
Advice/counselling	1	1	9	12
Campaigning	2	2	10	13
Charitable work	3	3	11	14
Community representation	4	4		15
Cultural activities	5	5		16
Education	6	6		17
Fund-raising	7	7		18
Publishing	8	8		19
Support for the elderly	9	9		20
Women's issues	10	10		21
Worship/meditation	11	11		22
Youth work	12	12		23
Other (please specify)	13	13	24 OTHER	25

6a. Is your organisation an "umbrella"/co-ordinating body to which other organisations are affiliated?

    Yes 1   No 2   If NO go to Section B: "Your Members"

6b. How many other organisations are affiliated to your organisation?

SECTION B: YOUR MEMBERS

In the following questions, we would like to ask you about the individuals in your organisation or the organisations that you represent.

7. Approximately how many individual members are in your organisation or in the organisations that you represent?

8. Please describe the main ethnic or "racial" background of the members of your organisation.

Guidance for completion of sections C to M

■ In the following sections we would like you to answer questions about the experiences of individuals in your organisation. Please answer as best you can to reflect the experiences and views of your members.

■ If your organisation is a **national** or "**umbrella**" organisation for other groups and movements please answer as **best** you can to reflect their views and experiences.

■ As the enclosed leaflet describes, the research will also collect direct evidence on the experiences and views of individuals through fieldwork and interviews across England and Wales.

■ Specifically, we would like to know whether you think your members are treated unfairly because of their religion. This could happen because of the attitudes or behaviour of other people (e.g. ignorance or hostility) or because the policies and/or practices of organisations give rise to unfair treatment.

■ We are also interested in finding out what, if any, differences there are between the formal policies of organisations and what they actually do in practice. In some areas the question therefore separates policies and practices. By **policies** we mean formally stated commitments that have some effect on religious groups, whether or not this was the intention. By **practices** we mean the actions of such organisations in reality.

  - Where organisations have formal policies that you know disadvantage members of your religion, please tick "yes frequently" or "yes occasionally" next to policies.

  - Where the policies do not cause unfair treatment, or are intended to avoid unfair treatment, please tick "no unfair treatment".

  - If you do not know whether the organisations concerned have any formal policies that might affect members of your religion, please tick "no experience in this area".

■ A further concern is to gather information on the nature of any unfair treatment and to learn more about the ways in which unfair treatment on the basis of religion may overlap with "racial"/ethnic discrimination for certain groups.

SECTION C: EDUCATION

9. Do your members, or their children, experience unfair treatment because of their religion in any of the following areas?

	Yes frequently	Yes occasionally	No unfair treatment	No experience in this area	
	1	2	3	4	
Schools					
Attitudes/behaviour of teachers					32
Attitudes/behaviour of pupils					33
Policies of schools					34
Practices of schools					35
Religious education curriculum					36
Religious education teaching					37
Teaching of Citizenship Studies					38
Collective worship arrangements					39
Other (Please write in below)					40 OTHER 41
Universities and colleges					
Attitudes/behaviour of staff					42
Attitudes/behaviour of students					43
Policies of universities/colleges					44
Practices of universities/colleges					45
Education authorities					
Attitudes/behaviour of officials					46
Policies of education authorities					47
Practices of education authorities					48
Other agencies involved in education (Please write in below)					49 OTHER 50

If you have not ticked 'yes' to any of these questions, please go to section D.

51-53

10. *a)* Where possible, please give a specific example of this unfair treatment.

54-56

10. *b)* Can you suggest any ways in which this problem could be tackled? If you are aware of an example of good practice, you may wish to mention this.

	FOR OFFICE USE ONLY

SECTION D: EMPLOYMENT

11. Do your members experience unfair treatment because of their religion in any of the following areas?

	Yes frequently	Yes occasionally	No unfair treatment	No experience in this area
	1	2	3	4
Private sector employers				
57 Attitudes/behaviour of managers	☐	☐	☐	☐
58 Attitudes/behaviour of colleagues	☐	☐	☐	☐
59 Policies of private sector employers	☐	☐	☐	☐
60 Practices of private sector employers	☐	☐	☐	☐
Public sector employers				
61 Attitudes/behaviour of managers	☐	☐	☐	☐
62 Attitudes/behaviour of colleagues	☐	☐	☐	☐
63 Policies of public sector employers	☐	☐	☐	☐
64 Practices of public sector employers	☐	☐	☐	☐
Voluntary sector employers				
65 Attitudes/behaviour of managers	☐	☐	☐	☐
66 Attitudes/behaviour of colleagues	☐	☐	☐	☐
67 Policies of voluntary sector employers	☐	☐	☐	☐
68 Practices of voluntary sector employers	☐	☐	☐	☐
The Employment Service				
69 Attitudes/behaviour of Jobcentre staff	☐	☐	☐	☐
70 Policies of Jobcentres	☐	☐	☐	☐
71 Practices of Jobcentres	☐	☐	☐	☐
Private employment agencies				
72 Attitudes/behaviour of staff	☐	☐	☐	☐
73 Policies of private agencies	☐	☐	☐	☐
74 Practices of private agencies	☐	☐	☐	☐
Other employment				
75 76 OTHER Please write in below	☐	☐	☐	☐

If you have not ticked 'yes' to any of these questions, please go to section E.

77-79

12. a) Where possible, please give a specific example of this unfair treatment.

80-82

12. b) Can you suggest any ways in which this problem could be tackled? If you are aware of an example of good practice, you may wish to mention this.

SECTION E. HOUSING

13. Do your members experience unfair treatment because of their religion in any of the following areas?

	Yes frequently	Yes occasionally	No unfair treatment	No experience in this area
	1	2	3	4

Owning or buying a house

Attitudes/behaviour of estate agents — 83

Policies/practices of estate agents — 84

Attitudes/behaviour of neighbours — 85

Renting from a private landlord

Attitudes/behaviour of private landlords — 86

Policies/practices of private landlords — 87

Attitudes/behaviour of lettings agents — 88

Policies/practices of lettings agents — 89

Attitudes/behaviour of other tenants — 90

Renting from the council

Attitudes or behaviour of council staff — 91

Policies of councils — 92

Practices of councils — 93

Attitudes/behaviour of other tenants — 94

Policies/practices of tenants' associations — 95

Renting from housing associations/trusts

Attitudes/behaviour of staff — 96

Policies of associations/trusts — 97

Practices of associations/trusts — 98

Attitudes/behaviour of other tenants — 99

Policies/practices of tenants' associations — 100

Other agencies involved in housing
Please write in below

101 OTHER   102

If you have not ticked 'yes' to any of these questions, go to section F.

14. *a)* Where possible, please give a specific example of this unfair treatment.

103-105

106-108

14. *b)* Can you suggest any ways in which this problem could be tackled? If you are aware of an example of good practice, you may wish to mention this.

	FOR OFFICE USE ONLY

SECTION F. HEALTH

15. Do your members experience unfair treatment because of their religion in any of the following areas?

	Yes frequently 1	Yes occasionally 2	No unfair treatment 3	No experience in this area 4
NHS surgeries and health centres				
Attitudes/behaviour of GPs or other medical staff	☐	☐	☐	☐
Attitudes/behaviour of non-medical staff	☐	☐	☐	☐
Policies/practices of surgeries and health centres	☐	☐	☐	☐
NHS hospitals				
Attitudes/behaviour of medical staff	☐	☐	☐	☐
Attitudes/behaviour of non-medical staff	☐	☐	☐	☐
Attitudes/behaviour of patients	☐	☐	☐	☐
Policies of hospital trusts	☐	☐	☐	☐
Practices of hospital trusts	☐	☐	☐	☐
Private health care				
Attitudes/behaviour of medical staff	☐	☐	☐	☐
Attitudes/behaviour of non-medical staff	☐	☐	☐	☐
Attitudes/behaviour of patients	☐	☐	☐	☐
Policies/practices of private hospitals	☐	☐	☐	☐
Other health services Please write in below	☐	☐	☐	☐

If you have not ticked 'yes' to any of these questions, please go to section G.

16. *a)* Where possible, please give a specific example of this unfair treatment.

16. *b)* Can you suggest any ways in which this problem could be tackled? If you are aware of an example of good practice, you may wish to mention this.

Office use codes: 109, 110, 111, 112, 113, 114, 115, 116, 117, 118, 119, 120, 121 OTHER, 122, 123-125, 126-128

SECTION G: LAW AND CRIMINAL JUSTICE

17. Do your members experience unfair treatment because of their religion in any of the following areas?

	Yes frequently	Yes occasionally	No unfair treatment	No experience in this area	
	1	2	3	4	
Police					
Attitudes/behaviour of the police					129
Policies of the police					130
Practices of the police					131
Legal services					
Attitudes/behaviour of lawyers					132
Attitudes/behaviour of court or tribunal staff					133
Policies/practices of courts/tribunals					134
Prison service					
Attitudes/behaviour of prison staff					135
Attitudes/behaviour of prison inmates					136
Policies of prisons					137
Practices of prisons					138
Probation service					
Attitudes/behaviour of probation staff					139
Policies of the probation service					140
Practices of the probation service					141
Immigration service					
Attitudes/behaviour of immigration staff					142
Policies of the immigration service					143
Practices of the immigration service					144

Other legal and criminal justice services
Please write in below

145
OTHER
146

If you have not ticked 'yes' to any of these questions, please go to section H.

18. a) Where possible, please give a specific example of this unfair treatment.

147-149

18. b) Can you suggest any ways in which this problem could be tackled? If you are aware of an example of good practice, you may wish to mention this.

150-152

SECTION H: OTHER SERVICES

19. Do your members experience unfair treatment because of their religion in any of the following areas?

	Yes frequently [1]	Yes occasionally [2]	No unfair treatment [3]	No experience in this area [4]
Social services				
Attitudes/behaviour of social services staff	☐	☐	☐	☐
Policies of social services departments	☐	☐	☐	☐
Practices of social services departments	☐	☐	☐	☐
Benefits Agency				
Attitudes/behaviour of Benefits Agency staff	☐	☐	☐	☐
Policies/practices of the Benefits Agency	☐	☐	☐	☐
Local authority planning services				
Attitudes/behaviour of planners	☐	☐	☐	☐
Policies of the planning authority	☐	☐	☐	☐
Practices of the planning authority	☐	☐	☐	☐
Local authority leisure services				
Attitudes/behaviour of staff	☐	☐	☐	☐
Policies of the leisure services department	☐	☐	☐	☐
Practices of the leisure services department	☐	☐	☐	☐
Public transport				
Attitudes/behaviour of public transport staff	☐	☐	☐	☐
Policies/practices of public transport providers	☐	☐	☐	☐
Shops and stores				
Attitudes/behaviour of shop staff	☐	☐	☐	☐
Attitudes/behaviour of other customers	☐	☐	☐	☐
Policies/practices of shops or stores	☐	☐	☐	☐
Other services Please write in below	☐	☐	☐	☐

If you have not ticked 'yes' to any of these questions, please go to section I.

20. *a)* Where possible, please give a specific example of this unfair treatment.

20. *b)* Can you suggest any ways in which this problem could be tackled? If you are aware of an example of good practice, you may wish to mention this.

SECTION I: FUNDING BODIES In this section, we are specifically interested in the experiences of your organisation, rather than individual members.

21. Does your organisation ever experience unfair treatment because of religion when applying for funding in any of the following areas?

	Yes frequently	Yes occasionally	No unfair treatment	No experience in this area	
	1	2	3	4	
Charities and trusts					
Attitudes/behaviour of staff					177
Policies of charities/trusts					178
Practices of charities/trusts					179
Local government					
Attitudes/behaviour of staff responsible for funding					180
Policies in relation to funding					181
Practices in relation to funding					182
Central government					
Attitudes/behaviour of staff responsible for funding					183
Policies in relation to funding					184
Practices in relation to funding					185
Public donation					
Attitudes/behaviour of the general public					186
Other sources of funding Please write in below					
				187 OTHER	188

If you have not ticked 'yes' to any of these questions, go to section J.

22. a) Where possible, please give a specific example of this unfair treatment.

189-191

22. b) Can you suggest any ways in which this problem could be tackled? If you are aware of an example of good practice, you may wish to mention this.

192-194

SECTION J: THE MEDIA In this section, we are specifically interested in your experiences of the media. In particular we are interested in the experiences of both your organisation and of your religious community generally.

23. How often, if ever, does your organisation or religious community experience unfair treatment because of their religion in any of the following areas?

	Yes frequently 1	Yes occasionally 2	No unfair treatment 3	No experience in this area 4
National Newspapers/Magazines Attitudes/behaviour of journalists	☐	☐	☐	☐
Coverage of your organisation	☐	☐	☐	☐
Coverage of your religion	☐	☐	☐	☐
Local Newspapers/Magazines Attitudes/behaviour of journalists	☐	☐	☐	☐
Coverage of your organisation	☐	☐	☐	☐
Coverage of your religion	☐	☐	☐	☐
National Radio Attitudes/behaviour of journalists or presenters	☐	☐	☐	☐
Coverage of your organisation	☐	☐	☐	☐
Coverage of your religion	☐	☐	☐	☐
Local Radio Attitudes/behaviour of journalists or presenters	☐	☐	☐	☐
Coverage of your organisation	☐	☐	☐	☐
Coverage of your religion	☐	☐	☐	☐
Television Attitudes/behaviour of journalists or presenters	☐	☐	☐	☐
Coverage of your organisation	☐	☐	☐	☐
Coverage of your religion	☐	☐	☐	☐
Other aspects of the media Please write in below	☐	☐	☐	☐

If you have not ticked 'yes' to any of these questions, please go to section K.

24. a) Where possible, please give a specific example of this unfair treatment.

24. b) Can you suggest any ways in which this problem could be tackled? If you are aware of an example of good practice, you may wish to mention this.

FOR OFFICE USE ONLY

195
196
197
198
199
200
201
202
203
204
205
206
207
208
209
210 OTHER   211
212-214
215-217

SECTION K: OTHER RELIGIOUS MOVEMENTS/GROUPS

In this section we are interested in any unfair treatment your organisation or its members have experienced from other religious groups.

25. Has your organisation or its members experienced unfair treatment from other religious groups? Please tick appropriate box

218

1 ☐ Yes

2 ☐ No   (if NO go to section L)

26. Which religious group(s) are these?

219-221

27. Where possible, please provide a specific example of this unfair treatment

222-224

28. Can you suggest any ways in which this problem could be tackled? If you are aware of an example of good practice, you may wish to mention this.

225-227

SECTION L: NON-RELIGIOUS GROUPS In this section we are interested in any unfair treatment your organisation or its members have experienced from non-religious groups (eg political groups, community or pressure groups).

29. Has your organisation or its members experienced unfair treatment from non-religious groups? Please tick appropriate box

228

1 ☐ Yes

2 ☐ No (If NO go to section M)

30. Which non-religious group(s) are these?

229-231

31. Where possible, please provide a specific example of this unfair treatment

232-234

32. Can you suggest any ways in which this problem could be tackled? If you are aware of an example of good practice, you may wish to mention this.

235-237

	FOR OFFICE USE ONLY	

SECTION M: YOUR PERSONAL VIEW In this final section, we would like to ask you about your personal views on the nature of unfair treatment on the basis of religion.

33. Overall, how serious do you think the following problems/experiences are for people within your religion?

		very serious	quite serious	not at all serious	don't know
		1	2	3	4
238	Ignorance	☐	☐	☐	☐
239	Indifference	☐	☐	☐	☐
240	Hostility	☐	☐	☐	☐
241	Verbal abuse	☐	☐	☐	☐
242	Physical abuse	☐	☐	☐	☐
243	Damage to property	☐	☐	☐	☐
244	Policies of organisations	☐	☐	☐	☐
245	Practices of organisations	☐	☐	☐	☐
246	General coverage in the media	☐	☐	☐	☐

34. Over the last five years, do you think these problems/experiences of religious discrimination have become more or less frequent?

		more frequent	less frequent	stayed the same	don't know
		1	2	3	4
247	Ignorance	☐	☐	☐	☐
248	Indifference	☐	☐	☐	☐
249	Hostility	☐	☐	☐	☐
250	Verbal abuse	☐	☐	☐	☐
251	Physical abuse	☐	☐	☐	☐
252	Damage to property	☐	☐	☐	☐
253	Policies of organisations	☐	☐	☐	☐
254	Practices of organisations	☐	☐	☐	☐
255	General coverage in the media	☐	☐	☐	☐

35. How far do you think that in your religion ethnic or "racial" grounds are part of the reason for unfair treatment on the basis of religion?
Please tick appropriate box

256	Ethnic/"racial" grounds are not part of the reason	1 ☐
	Ethnic/"racial" grounds are a small part of the reason	2 ☐
	Ethnic/"racial" grounds are a large part of the reason	3 ☐
	Ethnic/"racial" grounds are the main reason	4 ☐
	Don't know	5 ☐

36. Please use the space below for any further comments you may have on how far, if at all, you think ethnic or "racial" grounds are part of the reason for unfair treatment on the basis of religion.

257-259

37. Which of the following measures, if any, do you think should be considered in order to combat unfair treatment on the basis of religion? (Please tick up to **three**).

260-262

Take no new action   1

More teaching of comparative religion in schools   2

Policy reviews in each service area to promote equal treatment   3

Better training of staff/employees   4

Public education programmes   5

Voluntary codes of practice   6

Changes in the law/Introduce new law   7

Other (Please specify)   8

263
OTHER

264-266

38. If you have any other comments about unfair treatment on the basis of religion or suggestions for combating it, please use the space below.

CONTACT DETAILS: The following information will ensure that we do not send reminders to organisations that have already responded, and will enable us to contact you if there are any queries. No organisations or individuals responding to the questionnaire will be identified in the results or report of the project.

Name of organisation: 267

Contact name: 268

Position: 269

Tel: 270

Thank you for your help with this research. Please return the completed questionnaire and feedback form by <u>March 24th 2000,</u> using the FREEPOST envelope provided.

Annex B   Technical report

This annex describes the main information gathering techniques and methodological decisions taken in carrying out the research, and gives further details on response rates to the postal survey. It also provides further background information on the organisations responding to the survey.

Postal survey

At the outset of the project, it was decided to send about 2,000 questionnaires to religious organisations. However, deriving a sample was beset with difficulties. What counts as a religious organisation? Were there listings of such organisations from which to sample? How would questionnaires be distributed between the different faith groups?

As discussed in the *Interim Report*, the definition of religion is problematic. The decision was taken to be as inclusive as possible. For some groups, the unwillingness of the rest of society to recognise their belief system as a religion is central to their claims of discrimination, and excluding them from the survey would have perpetuated this situation. However, this inclusiveness may mean that the sample frame contained a few groups who would prefer to describe their belief system as a philosophy or a way of life, and not necessarily as a religion.

It was clearly important to include the religions that are associated with ethnic minority groups in this country (although in practice, of course, religions such as Islam and Buddhism are multi-ethnic). Christian traditions were also included. This was partly because of the argument that in a society that is said to be dominated by secular values, those with a profoundly held belief in any religion can feel misunderstood and unfairly treated. It was also because there are some traditions identifying themselves as Christian whose beliefs and practices regularly attract criticism from the wider society.

Sources of information for the sample frames

There is no single definitive index of religious organisations in England and Wales. The main source used was *Religions in the UK: On-Line* (Weller, ed, 2000 at http://www.multifaithnet.org) which was last updated in spring 1999. This was supplemented by the inclusion of organisations that had supplied details to the team responsible for the database, but did not wish to appear in the on-line version. Additional information was then obtained from the Christian Research Association's *UK Christian Handbook* (Brierley and Wraight 1998/9); the *Muslim Directory Online*; the Information Network on New Religious Movements; and from some snowballing of contacts through various religious organisations themselves.

Attempts were also made to contact Chinese community organisations. Whilst some Chinese are practising Buddhists or Christians, there are also influences from the Confucian, Taoist and folk traditions which were not otherwise represented on the existing databases. Unfortunately, only a handful of such organisations completed questionnaires, and these mainly identified themselves as Buddhist.

The combined sources yielded listings for about 45,000 Christian organisations and 4,800 from other religions. In addition to faith group, information was available on the geographical region in which each organisation was located and whether the scope of its operations was mainly national, regional or local.

Sampling strategy

There were huge differences in the number of organisations available to be sampled: for example over 16,000 Anglican churches compared with 15 Zoroastrian organisations. Any attempt at proportional sampling would have resulted in the overwhelming majority of questionnaires going to a small number of Christian denominations, and a small handful to most of the other traditions. It was decided instead to send questionnaires to all the known national organisations in each religion and to try to top this up with local organisations so that no individual tradition was sent fewer than 50 questionnaires in total. Given the target response rate of 60 per cent, this would have ensured at least 30 responses from any one group.

The various Christian denominations were treated as separate traditions for this purpose. In the case of several numerically large minority faiths (Buddhism, Hinduism, Islam, Judaism and Sikhism) the target number of questionnaires was increased to between 100 and 300, very broadly in line with estimated membership[6].

The sample for each religion was stratified to ensure that Wales and the English regions, and the level at which organisations operated (regional or local) were represented according to the proportions left in the sample frame after extracting the national

---

6   See the *Interim Report* for estimated numbers and a discussion of the difficulties involved in estimating 'active' and 'community' membership. Because inclusion of 93 national Jewish organisations left little scope for local organisations, the Jewish sample was further increased from 100 to 150.

organisations. Further stratification was applied to some sampling lists in order to ensure that the samples would be representative of the various distinct movements within each religious tradition. Organisations were then selected randomly from within each stratum.

The types of organisation included in the sample frames were places of worship and meditation, 'umbrella bodies', and single issue agencies concerned, for example, with care of the elderly, women's issues or youth work. As confirmed by subsequent analysis of the questionnaires, most organisations had multiple functions.

In practice, it did not prove possible to identify 50 organisations in every tradition and fewer questionnaires were therefore despatched in some cases. The table below compares the actual number of questionnaires despatched with the target.

Table B.1: Number of questionnaires despatched compared with target

Religious tradition	Target	Actually despatched	Of which: Local	Regional	National
Bahá'í	50	50	26	21	3
Buddhist	100	100	38	4	58
Chinese	50	29	11	13	5
Christian	669	637	518	0	119
Christian (other)	100	80	66	0	14
Hindu	100	100	64	2	34
Jain	50	41	21	10	10
Jewish	150	150	56	1	93
Muslim	300	300	145	1	154
NRM/Pagan	100	100	12	0	88
Sikh	100	100	73	1	26
Zoroastrian	50	15	0	13	2
Inter-faith	108	108	76	0	32 [7]
Other	20	20	15	0	5
Total	1,947	1,830	1,121	66	643

---

7   Includes a number of organisations with a combined national and international remit.

The composition of the Christian sample was as follows:

Tradition	Target	Despatched
National	119	119
Anglican	50	50
Baptist	50	50
Black led	50	47
Ecumenical	50	50
Independent	50	50
Methodist	50	50
New Church	50	45
Orthodox	50	46
Pentecostal	50	50
Presbyterian	50	30
Roman Catholic	50	50

Questionnaire development

This was believed to be the first survey of its kind. The design of the questionnaire was informed by surveys of racial discrimination and of religious belief, by comparable postal surveys of organisations, and by survey research on religious discrimination carried out in Northern Ireland.

The aim was to gather as much information as possible about the level and nature of religious discrimination (defined very broadly as 'unfair treatment' for survey purposes); the degree of overlap between religious and racial discrimination; and the policy options that respondents thought might be effective in reducing discrimination. Although there were a large number of 'tick box' questions, an attempt was made via the open-ended questions to gather respondents' own specific examples of unfair treatment and any specific suggestions for ways in which it might be overcome.

Pilot

The questionnaire was piloted with 125 organisations, chosen to reflect a range of religions and with variations in function, scope and geographical location. This was an opportunity to review a number of issues relating to the detailed implementation of the survey, as well as the design of the questionnaire itself. In particular, it was important to consider the very varied size, nature and resources of the target organisations.

The main problem identified by the pilot was the need for a variety of measures to maximise the response (see below). Improvements were also made to the design and layout of the questionnaire, and there was some fine-tuning of the questions.

Main stage

Questionnaires were despatched in early February 2000 with a return date of 24 March, although this period was subsequently extended.

Measures taken to enhance the response

Partly as a result of the pilot, a number of measures were put in place to try and encourage as many organisations as possible to participate in the survey:

- many of the addresses for small, local organisations were checked before despatch in order to minimise the number of questionnaires that went to organisations that had moved or ceased to exist
- envelopes were marked to be returned to the University of Derby if undelivered
- the despatch was timed to avoid any major religious holidays
- the covering letter contained summaries in Arabic, Gujarati, Hindi, Punjabi, Urdu and Welsh and gave a telephone number to ring if respondents required assistance in another language. Provision was then made for re-contacting them.
- as many organisations as possible were contacted by phone to check the arrival of the materials and to encourage a response
- postcard reminders were sent to non-respondents, followed by further telephone calls, many of which were made by people with a variety of language skills
- emails were used to chase the response where contact addresses were available
- notices were carried in a number of inter-faith and religious newspapers, magazines and newsletters. Religious organisations contacting the project were asked to encourage a response from within their own communities
- organisations declining to complete a questionnaire were contacted again and encouraged, when appropriate, to participate
- organisations contacted in the course of interviewing in the four case study areas were encouraged to respond if they had received a questionnaire
- the deadline for response was extended in order to give organisations more time for internal consultations, or for key staff to become available.

Various steps were also taken to raise the profile and general awareness of the research. A large number of leaflets were distributed explaining the terms of reference and a website was established through the University of Derby MultiFaithNet internet service. There was also a fair degree of media coverage of the project, especially around the time the interim report was published, which coincided with the despatch of questionnaires.

Data preparation

The data were input by a team in the University of Derby Religious Resource and Research Centre, using SPSS 8 software under the supervision of Dr. Kingsley Purdam and Ahmed Andrews, and were rigorously and extensively checked for inputting errors. All entered cases were re-checked for accuracy. Responses to the open-ended questions were coded manually using coding frames developed from an analysis of a sample of the verbatim comments. Anonymised data from the survey is now held by the Home Office.

Response rates

From the total of 1,830 questionnaires despatched, 628 were returned and 77 organisations declined to participate. Some of the remaining organisations who failed to respond to the survey had ceased to exist or moved away. Others could not be reached on the phone, or were contacted but failed to return a questionnaire by the extended deadline. The local organisational scene among minority groups is often very fluid with organisations coming into existence and disbanding quite rapidly, and it was not always possible to clarify whether an organisation was still in existence.

Organisations that have ceased to exist or moved without trace constitute 'deadwood' and are conventionally removed from the count of despatched questionnaires before calculating response rates. Some deadwood was fairly easy to identify – for example because envelopes were returned marked 'gone away' and telephone enquiries failed to trace the organisation.

In other cases the position was less clear cut. Some of the smaller organisations did not have any permanent staff or publicly advertised telephone numbers. It has therefore been necessary in table B.2 below to give a range for the response rate rather than a precise figure. The lower figure represents the number of completed questionnaires divided by the number sent out; the higher figure the number of completed questionnaires divided by the number sent out after allowing for *both* known deadwood *and* for organisations whose staff could not be contacted. The actual response rates for each religion will be somewhere within the ranges given and are unlikely to be at either extreme.

Table B.2   *Response rates*

Religious tradition	Sent out	Deadwood and other non-contact	Refused	Completed	Response rate
Bahá'í	50	9	2	25	50-61%
Buddhist	100	11	8	33	33-37%
Chinese	29	3	6	7	24-27%
Christian	717	98	8	311	43-50%
National orgs	119	13	7	33	28-31%
Orthodox	46	11	0	9	20-26%
Methodist	50	0	0	27	54%
Baptist	50	6	0	24	48-55%
Ecumenical	50	5	0	27	54-60%
Black-led	47	7	0	15	32-38%
Pentecostal	50	6	0	23	46-52%
Roman Catholic	50	11	0	20	40-51%
Presbyterian	30	8	0	6	20-27%
New Church	45	6	0	21	47-54%
Independent	50	5	0	25	50-56%
Anglican	50	5	1	27	54-60%
Other	80	10	0	54	68-77%
Hindu	100	27	3	37	37-51%
Inter-faith	108	14	14	27	25-29%
Jain	41	16	4	7	17-28%
Jewish	150	39	15	40	27-36%
Muslim	300	65	6	70	23-30%
NRM/Pagan	100	21	4	27	27-34%
Sikh	100	23	2	35	35-45%
Zoroastrian	15	3	1	7	47-58%
Other	20	5	4	2	10-13%
Total	1,830	329	77	628	34-42%

Possible reasons for non-response

Whilst not unusual for a postal survey, most of these response rates were lower than the target of 60 per cent set at the outset of the research. Some of the factors that may have contributed to this are discussed below.

Religious discrimination not an issue?

It is possible that a low response indicates lack of concern about religious discrimination. However, the response rates for individual religions do not seem to bear very much relationship to the concern about religious discrimination expressed by those who did respond. For example the response from Muslim organisations was relatively low, yet those who did respond were more likely to claim unfair treatment of their members than other religions. Some (but not all) of the highest response rates came from groups with fewer claims of unfair treatment. As mentioned later in this Annex, some people were reluctant to discuss painful and sensitive issues.

Questionnaire design

The length and complexity of the questionnaire may have deterred some organisations from preparing a response. The 'tick box' design facilitates rapid completion, but it may have appeared very repetitive and/or simplistic.

Linguistic and cultural barriers

The language and concepts used in the questionnaire may have failed to resonate with some groups, even where the use of English as opposed to other languages was not in itself a barrier. Some of the lowest response rates came from religious groups that are also associated with ethnic minorities.

'Hard to reach' groups

Some religious groups may regard both the practice of religion and the issues raised by the research to be extremely personal and private, or they may not have wished to engage with state-sponsored research.

National v local perspectives

It was expected at the outset that small local organisations might be less likely to respond than national organisations, either because they do not have the resources to devote to completing questionnaires, or because they may have less of an 'axe to grind' than national lobby groups. It was also expected that they would be harder to contact. In fact the response from local groups (1,121 questionnaires despatched and 458 returned) appears to have been better than that from national organisations (643 questionnaires despatched and 154 returned). One reason for this may be the vicarious nature of the questionnaire: small local organisations may have found it easier to generalise about the experiences of their membership than large national bodies.

However, there was also a wide variation between religions in the ratio of national to local organisations in the sample frames and in the samples actually selected (table B.1). A low response from national organisations could have 'caused' (or at least contributed) to the low response from some religions, or vice versa. Within most religions, the percentage of questionnaires that were returned was in fact broadly similar for both local and national organisations. The main exception was in the large Christian sample, where it was 47 per cent for the local organisations compared with only 26 per cent for national organisations. Two other religions (Judaism and Islam) contributed a relatively large number of national organisations to the sample. In both these cases the percentage of national and local organisations that returned questionnaires was similar, but the low response rate for the religion as a whole will have contributed to the low overall response from national organisations.

Responses to individual questions

Throughout the main body of the questionnaire, respondents were given the option of saying that they did not have enough experience of the area concerned to offer an opinion on the frequency of unfair treatment. This meant that the number of organisations answering individual questions varied considerably. Some of the questions on education or the media, for example, were answered by a large majority in all religions. As might be expected, questions about areas such as the probation service, prisons and private health care attracted the smallest number of answers. For a few traditions, such questions were answered by fewer than one in five of potential respondents.

Background information on respondent organisations

Table B.3 below shows the scope of operation of the organisations that responded to the survey.

Table B.3   Scope of operation

	Local	Regional	National	Total
Bahá'í	13	11	1	25
Buddhist	15	0	18	33
Christian	277	0	34	311
Hindu	25	1	11	37
Jain	4	1	2	7
Jewish	15	1	24	40
Muslim	31	0	39	70
NRM/Pagan	26	0	1	27
Sikh	24	0	11	35
Zoroastrian	5	0	2	7
Inter-faith	20	0	7	27
Chinese	1	2	4	7
Other	2	0	0	2
Total	458	16	154	628

Overall, the national and local organisations within each religion gave similar answers in response to the questionnaire. The main exception to this was Muslim organisations, where national organisations were generally somewhat more likely to report unfair treatment than local organisations. The text draws attention to those instances where local/national disparities were greatest.

Region

Table B.4 opposite shows the region in which respondent organisations were located. The relatively high proportion of organisations representing minority religions that were located in London is likely to result both from the presence of many national organisations and the relative concentration of minority groups in the capital.

Membership

Table B.5 below gives membership numbers for those organisations that provided this information. 35 per cent had between 101 and 1,000 members and another 28 per cent had 26-100 members. 20 per cent claimed over 2,500.

Table B.4: Geographic location of respondent organisations

Religious tradition	North East	Yorkshire	North West	East Midlands	West Midlands	East Anglia	Greater London	South East	South West	Wales	Total
Bahá'í	1	2	2	1	1	1	5	7	3	2	25
Buddhist		1	3	2	6	1	8	5	3	4	33
Christian	19	29	31	31	33	17	48	38	32	33	311
Hindu		3	1	8	4		14	6		1	37
Jain							7				7
Jewish	1	1	4	1	1		32				40
Muslim		7	4	10	9	1	33	3	2	1	70
NRM/Pagan		1	2		3	1	6	10	3	1	27
Sikh	1	1	1	5	11		10	3	3		35
Zoroastrian	1	1	2				2				6
Inter-faith	2	1	1	3	3	1	8	2	5	1	27
Chinese			2		1		4				7
Selected other				1		1					2
Total	25	47	53	62	72	23	177	74	51	43	627

Table B.5: Membership of respondent organisations

Religious tradition	Number of members					
	1-25	26-100	101-1000	1001-2500	2500+	Total
Bahá'í	18	4			3	25
Buddhist	6	6	8	1	6	27
Christian	7	112	98	16	45	278
Hindu	1	3	18	6	6	34
Jain		1	2		3	6
Jewish	3	3	13	1	13	33
Muslim	10	9	22	4	11	56
NRM/pagan	2	2	4	1	9	18
Sikh	5	3	14	5	5	32
Zoroastrian	1	2	2		1	6
Inter-faith	4	8	6	1	4	23
Chinese	1	1	3			5
Selected other					2	2
Total	58	154	190	35	108	545

Umbrella bodies

Nearly a quarter of the respondent organisations were umbrella bodies. As might be expected from the ratio of national to local organisations, the proportion of umbrella organisations was higher for minority religions (29 per cent) than for the Christian sample (16 per cent). Across the whole sample, 37 per cent of the national organisations described themselves as 'umbrella' compared with 18 per cent of the local organisations.

100 of the umbrella bodies provided information on the number of organisations that were affiliated to them. Nearly two thirds (63) put this number at 25 or fewer and another 22 at between 26 and 100.

Field Interviews

Locations

Based upon the Religious Resource and Research Centre's knowledge of the religious landscape in England and Wales, four city locations were selected for more detailed study. They were chosen to take into account the various different population characteristics and balances across the four areas. Research was carried out in the following locales for approximately six weeks in each during 1999/2000: Leicester (November-December 1999), the London Borough of Newham, (January-February 2000), Blackburn (March-April 2000), and Cardiff (May-June 2000).

Methodological issues

Narratives and "giving voice"

In researching the nature, extent, and patterns of religious discrimination and the possible measures for combating it, it was important that the fieldwork should "give voice" to previously unheard and/or marginalised perspectives, thus enabling these voices and experiences to contribute to the public and political debates around these issues. Personal narratives play an important role when considering policy options. For policy to be effective, it needs to be grounded in the experiences and worldview of those most likely to be affected.

The changing shape of qualitative research

Both within academic discourse and community politics, there has been an emerging critique of conventional assumptions that a researcher can systematically discover and interpret in a value-free way, the stories and experience of those who are seen as the passive objects of the research process.

One of the main effects of such developments has been to transform the roles of researcher and researched, so that those who are researched are no longer the objects of study to be theorised about but are themselves also seen and acknowledged as experts and authorities, as participants in, and co-creators of the inquiry itself, to whom the researcher should acknowledge an appropriate accountability. At the same time, the consideration of appropriate criteria remain important for the planning and conduct of the research, as well as for consideration of its results. Therefore, through the way in which its fieldwork was planned and conducted, as well as in the presentation of findings derived from it, the project sought to embody the criteria of reliability and trustworthiness.

Reliability

In terms of conventional scientific research, reliability is concerned with the stability of the research methods that are used and the findings that are derived from them. It indicates the validity, accuracy and truthfulness of any research findings. However, the current academic and political debates around the politics of knowledge production and representation, as referred to above, underline that, whilst the criteria of reliability and trustworthiness remain, their interpretation and meaning needs to be transformed in a way that takes account of the shifting nature of field settings and the fact that inquiries like the Religious Discrimination in England and Wales Research Project cannot be viewed as neutral.

First of all, the project's funding by Government inevitably had a significant impact, both for good and ill, upon both perceptions of the project, and participation in it. Secondly, the location of the researchers in a University rather than a community context also has its inevitable impact on the relationships involved in the research. Thirdly, the individuals and groups who are researched are themselves actors in a political process in which they are seeking to advance various views, interests and perspectives rather than just to comment in a detached way on the existing situation.

However, to recognise this does not mean that the goals of rigour and of valid, systematic inquiry are abandoned. At the same time, if conventional notions of neutrality, objectivity and validity are flawed, then this does mean that the notion of reliability within qualitative research needs to be modified.

Trustworthiness

Personal experience research permits researchers to enter into the social world of the researched in ways that are rooted in the formation of relationships. Therefore, whilst personal experience research methods must answer to standards of rigour and systematicity, they must also be accountable for the consequences of the relationships that are initiated and developed in the context of the research process. As feminist researchers have expressed it, in graphic imagery, anything other than such accountability would be akin to "research as rape". This relates to the criteria of "trustworthiness" which is of importance, in different ways, to both the producers and the consumers of research. Such "trustworthiness" is linked with credibility, with the potential for transferability and the possibility of confirmability.

Credibility

Credibility is one of the most important aspects of trustworthiness – once again, this is so both from the perspective of those who have been researched, and also those who are consumers of the research findings. Credibility relates to the level of confidence that both researched subjects and the consumers of research can have in the compatibility between what is attributed to participants and that which they intend. It is also linked with the need, where these exist, for the representation of research findings adequately to present perspectives that both converge and diverge. What is produced in this way is more often a mosaic image than a systematic record. It is often not too precise in terms of definition, but can be very rich in terms of meaning and value.

Transferability

The potential transferability of a study's finding is a key dimension of its possibility for being implemented. In the case of qualitative research, this is not achieved by random sampling techniques across a given population to enable generalisability of results to take place. Rather, qualitative research seeks to provide as much detailed information as possible about specific contexts. While the result of this is that the findings are inevitably context-specific, the level and richness of what is documented by the research can enable the making of "working hypotheses" to inform further inquiry and or the applicability of findings to policy-making decisions.

Fieldwork planning: types of interviews and selection of interviewees

The major aim of the fieldwork, as one methodological dimension of the project's mixed model design, was to provide the means for contextualising and grounding the issues with which the project has been concerned. It sought to do this by addressing the issues concerned with the everyday life and environs of individuals, groups, communities and organisations. In doing this, it aimed to enrich the languages through which the issues of unfair treatment on the basis of religion, and the possible steps for tackling this, might be articulated, discussed and debated.

The selection – both among religious communities and wider, "secular" agencies was based upon the need to select individuals and groups who could:

- speak to the aims of the project
- provide comment upon evidence and patterns of religious discrimination
- reflect upon the larger issues and influences which shape and are shaped by experiences of religious discrimination.

A variety of different techniques were drawn upon in order to try to ensure the trustworthiness of the research and its findings. The fieldwork involved the following kinds of interviews.

Biographical interviews

Interviews were arranged with "ordinary individuals" who claimed to have experienced discrimination on the basis of religion. The inclusion of such interviews was planned in order to balance the contributions to the project that were to be made by organisational representatives or by individuals in the more "public" settings of larger groups. The contributions from representatives of organisations are affected by organisational interests, whereas individuals are more free to express all the ambiguities of a particular experience or issue. In addition, the experience of discrimination can be extremely wounding to the degree that it can be very painful for those who have suffered it to open up in wider contexts. The individual biographical interviews therefore gave an opportunity for reporting on this level of individual experience.

Representatives of religious organisations

Given the limited time and resources of the project, and the four fieldwork locations to be covered, organisations were initially selected that function as "umbrella" organisations for their religion in the locality concerned. This, in turn, helped to facilitate other local organisational contacts for the religion concerned. In the case of some religions and some locations, it enabled the organisation of a group interview involving a number of representative members of the organisations affiliated to the "umbrella" group.

Advice agencies and other relevant groups/representatives

The questionnaire survey was only of religious organisations. The fieldwork's inclusion of institutions, organisations and groups constituted on an other than religious basis was therefore an important complementary aspect of the project. The first group of such organisations was those organisations which might be expected to offer a supportive or advice role to people with claims of discrimination. Thus Citizens' Advice Bureaux, Law Centres and Race Equality Councils were included.

Special and "single-issue" groups

The formation of focus groups based on professional recruitment was beyond the financial resources of the project. However, the fieldwork was able to draw upon the views and experience of a range of sectoral groups from the general public, such as youth and women's groups. Interviews with these groups were included in order to try and ensure that possibly distinct perspectives from people with characteristics that might not be reflected among those whom religious or other organisations put forward as their official representatives would nevertheless be included in the fieldwork design.

Employers and service providers

The purpose of these interviews was to explore the dilemmas involved for organisations when dealing with the issues arising from religious diversity and unfair treatment on the basis of religion. Those involved included local authorities (both as large employers and also as service providers) and other public, private, and voluntary sector employers. Particularly included were bodies and organisations whose areas of work paralleled the sectors and areas covered by the questionnaire survey, especially including education, health, police, employment and the media.

Preparatory measures – religious groups and individuals

In relation to religious organisations purposive sampling was employed, based upon the knowledge capital of the University of Derby's Religious Resource and Research Centre and its long history of work on, and with, religious organisations in the United Kingdom, especially through its Multi-Faith Directory Research Project. This was supplemented by the use of local Yellow Pages Directories and other local community and inter-faith directories. For the Christian Churches, mailing lists were obtained from the local and/or regional organisations in the Christian tradition concerned. Referrals were also given from relevant national organisations.

The conduct of purposive sampling requires significant engagement with the researched communities and groups. Therefore tacit knowledge and emerging insights from the process of inquiry were also used. Planning for the fieldwork took place by obtaining and reading relevant materials relating to the religious and ethnic composition of each locality. Data sources that were both preliminary and supplemental to the conduct of the research were identified and drawn upon in order to provide a richer insight into the local communities. These included obtaining and reading pamphlets, leaflets and other literature produced by/about community programmes and models developed to respond to issues around religious discrimination and attending relevant meetings or other pertinent fora within the locality.

Alongside information gathering, initial contact was made with a range of individuals from key organisations in each locality (such as inter-faith organisations and groups, race equality councils, chambers of commerce) through which appropriate further local contacts were made leading to the drawing up of a schedule of interviews.

Finally, introductory letters were sent to religious organisations in each locality, enclosing a project leaflet to explain the background to the project, advising them of when the fieldwork was intended to take place in their locality; and explaining that the project's fieldworker might be in touch with them in connection with the project's fieldwork.

Selection of fieldwork interviews for religious groups and individuals

Within this overall approach, an attempt was made to ensure balance and breadth of the wide range of experience, perceptions and representations that characterise the varied local contexts of the fieldwork. The main groups to be covered across all areas were identified (Bahá'í, Buddhist, Christian – especially Roman Catholic, Christian-based – especially Jehovah's Witness, Hindu, Jewish, and Muslim. Together with this, other groups that might be larger and/or more significant in specific localities were identified (such as Jains in

Leicester and Jehovah's Witnesses in Blackburn). Finally, there was also an attempt to identify any other marginalised or peripheral groups in a locality, such as Unificationists and Mormons.

The initial identification of contacts was developed as the fieldwork progressed, especially with regard to the identification and setting up of meetings for the biographical interviews. This often required meeting community representatives and individuals face to face to discuss what was intended prior to any introductions being made.

Preparatory measures – advice, service agencies and employers

Lists of potential organisations were derived from directories provided by local authorities, together with information available on local authority websites, community directories, local newspapers, flyers and advertisements posted in community venues.

Introductory mailings were then sent out enclosing a covering letter and a project leaflet introducing the project and the fieldworker. These mailings were then built upon by telephone contact and through personal referrals obtained in the course of the fieldwork, as well as in the light of new information gained once working in a given area.

Selection of fieldwork interviews for advice and service agencies and employers

In selecting advice organisation interviews, a particular effort was made to seek out active race equality and other organisations oriented to the needs of minority ethnic communities. An attempt was also made for the selection to encompass as wide a range of community interests and dimensions as possible (for example, women and youth) as well as a wide range of services (for example, legal, mediation, community development). Organisations were also identified that seemed to be involved in developing particularly innovative programmes/initiatives in terms of outreach, anti-discrimination, and community empowerment. The organisations reflected a wide range of funding arrangements, from those that were either fully or partially funded by local or national government, through to those that were completely independent of state funding.

In selecting local authority interviews, standard lists of education, funding, planning, social services, health and other departments/agency contacts were sought out. These were supplemented by those departments or units that were unique to that particular local authority or reflective of its particular structure and/or history. In Wales, this included allotting some of the Cardiff interviews for meetings with those involved in devolved government at the level of the National Assembly.

In selecting employers for interview, the emphasis was placed on large public sector organisations that were likely to be employing a substantial number of people from each local community. A number of smaller, private employers proved to be reticent to participate. In order to try and compensate for this and in order to maximise the representation within the fieldwork of employers' dilemmas, interests and issues, representatives of business development organisations and business charities were interviewed. This drew not only upon their own knowledge of the relevant issues, but also drew upon their active involvement with, and knowledge of, local and regional employers and business leaders.

Conduct of the fieldwork

Thus, rather than undertaking in-depth case studies or extensive ethnographic work, neither of which were possible within the constraints of the project funding or timetable, the fieldwork sought to capture and depict a representative picture or mosaic. In total[8], 156 meetings with approximately 318 people were completed: Leicester (34 meetings with approximately 70 people); Newham (45 meetings with approximately 113 people); Blackburn (38 meetings with approximately 87 people); Cardiff (39 meetings with approximately 48 people).

Interviews by city and type of interview

The breakdown of interview meetings, by city and type of interview, were as follows:

City	Religious Organisations	Advice Organisations	Services/ Employers	Biographies[9]	Total
Blackburn	10	10	12	6	38
Cardiff	8	12	10	9	39
Leicester	11	9	10	4	34
Newham	11	12	12	10	45
TOTALS	40	43	44	29	156

8 Excluding informal orientation and introduction meetings with local inter-faith groups and contacts; extended telephone conversations; introductory meetings held in order to arrange and gain permission for formal interviews which potential participants declined to proceed with; meetings conducted across more than one session; meetings in which the participant did not turn up and/or which it was necessary to reschedule.

9 The category of biographies records the number of individual meetings in which also a total of four teenage sons/daughters were present and one son in his twenties. It should be noted that a lot of other personal experience/biographical information was additionally conveyed during the course of other interviews and meetings.

Interviews with religious groups

The breakdown of the 40 interviews with religious organisations was as follows:

Bahá'í	3
Buddhist	2
Christian	18
including:	
African	1
Anglican	1
Baptist	1
Black Majority	3
Ecumenical	4
Evangelical	1
Free Church	1
Mormon	1
Quaker	1
Roman Catholic	4
Hindu	4
Inter-Faith	1
Jain	1
Jewish	2
Muslim	4
Pagan	1
Sikh	3
Zoroastrian	1

Biographical Interviews

The breakdown of the 29 biographical interviews was as follows:

Bahá'í	2
Christian	8
including:	
Black Anglican	1
Black Majority	1
Gay	1
Indian	2
Jehovah's Witness	2
Roman Catholic	1
Hindu[10]	5
Inter-Faith	1
Jewish	1
Muslim	4
NRM (Unificationist)	1
Pagan	3
Sikh	3
Zoroastrian[11]	1

The age and gender of those interviewed was as follows:

	Males	Females
Teens	1	2
20s	2	2
30s	4	2
40s	7	5
50s	2	1
60s	1	0
Total	17	12

10 Two sons/daughters in teens/early twenties were present across the Hindu biographical interviews.
11 Three sons/daughters in teens/early twenties were present across the Zoroastrian biographical interviews.

Advice Organisations

The breakdown of the 43 interviews with advice organisations was as follows:

Business/Professional	4
Community development	3
Education	2
General advice	4
Legal/Rights	5
Mediation	3
Race Equality/Ethnic Minority	12
Victim support/police	2
Women's	3
Youth	5

Service Agencies/Employers

The breakdown of the 44 interviews with service agency/employer organisations was as follows:

Employers/Human Resources	4
Local Authority[12]	33
National Assembly (Wales)	3
Police	4

Recording and use of interview data

Most interview notes were hand-written by the field researcher, although a few were taped. Summaries from interviews were read and evaluated by the field researcher and by the wider research project team.

The examples and quotations selected for inclusion in the report were chosen on the basis of including experiences and viewpoints which, whilst varying in context and the way in which they are expressed, are informed by as wide a range of religions, social organisations and institutions as possible. Examples and quotations are cited to extent that they convey the fullness of a particular issue, experience or viewpoint. Thus the cited examples and quotations are grouped together thematically rather than by location, religion, or type of institution. This was done in order to try to convey the key or fundamental issues and problems identified during the field research, as well as to highlight ways forward that have been tried and/or are proposed for tackling these issues and problems.

---

12 Including planning, funding, social services, education, health, regeneration and social inclusion.

At the same time, although the issues highlighted are those which emerged as broader themes from the field research, it should not be assumed that all religious groups and individuals have experienced each issue or area of concern in an equal way. Therefore the text of each chapter also notes where an issue is something that may particularly affect a specific group or groups. Other factors that may have a bearing on the contribution made by a particular interviewee or interviewees are also noted.

Thus the examples and quotations used in the report are included on the basis that they are as broadly representative of the research as possible, yet detailed and specific enough in order to provide well-grounded, detailed and multi-level findings.

Additional project information gathering

Further background information for the research was gathered through contact with a range of key agencies including: the Commission for Racial Equality, the Inter Faith Network, the Inner Cities Religious Council, The Advisory, Conciliation and Arbitration Service, The National Secular Society and a range of national religious organisations.

The project's on-line and paper-based publicity materials invited submissions to the project of relevant materials, and a range of organisations and individuals made such submissions. The project's website contained an on-line questionnaire which was intended to offer a facility for members of the wider public to feed in their experience and concerns in order to inform the background to the project. Because it was available for free response statistical findings are not possible from the on-line questionnaire. It was, in any event, used much less frequently than originally anticipated. This may have been due to website navigational issues in respect of the website design. There is also a question about the degree to which – especially in respect of those religious groups with a substantial proportion of people from the visible minorities – there is adequate access available to information technology. However, the website in general proved invaluable for the project as a source to which the project could point enquirers, including in respect of the project's *Interim Report and Executive Summary* which remain on the project's website following the distribution of all hard copies.

In addition the project formally approached the following to contribute any relevant materials to the project: the Equal Opportunities Commission, The Office for National Statistics, Law Centres Federation, The National Association of Citizen's Advice Bureaux, the Law Society, the Lord Chancellor's Department, The Law Commission and the Trades Union Congress. Where appropriate comments and information given by these respondents has been included in the report findings.

Issues arising during the postal survey and local interviews

It should be noted that, during the course of the postal survey and the fieldwork, a number of issues became apparent concerning the subject matter of the research. First of all the topic was noted as being a highly sensitive one, and a number of people did not want to relive their troubles, or possibly cause further difficulties, by discussing them. This became particularly apparent in relation to attempts to set up field interviews to access individual biographies and during the telephone reminders that were conducted in relation to the postal survey.

Secondly, some expressed fears about whether there might be ulterior motives for conducting the research and that it might be used against them and/or their interests. Some resentment was also expressed that so often researchers or research organisations conduct research without reporting back to any of the individuals, organisations or communities that participated. A large number of people were also dismayed by their perception of a lack of action in relation to the extensive research that has already been conducted within their communities.

Finally, in the light of increasing community consultation initiatives, many communities and organisations felt overburdened by demands on their time to engage in such activities. Many also pointed out that they are expected to contribute an extensive amount of time, resources and expertise to consultative and research-based initiatives, but without any remuneration, recognition or formal employment in relevant capacities.

The project attempted to respond to concerns about the recognition of contributors' input by sending copies of the *Executive Summary of its Interim Report* to all those who participated in the field research. From the data base the project has set up it is proposed to send a summary of the project findings both to those who participated in the fieldwork and to organisations that responded to the project's postal survey.

Annex C

Explanatory notes

The tables in parts 1 and 2 give results from the postal survey for the topics covered in chapters 3 to 10. Part 1 provides data for the minority religions and for Christians as a whole. Part 2 provides data for the individual Christian traditions (the latter data excludes national organisations). Part 3 gives results for the question about the measures that need to be considered to combat unfair treatment on the basis of religion.

Parts 1 and 2

1. Most entries in the table represent the response of organisations from the religion concerned to the question: *Do your members[13] experience unfair treatment because of their religion in any of the following areas?* Respondents were asked to choose between four answer categories: *'yes frequently', 'yes occasionally', 'no unfair treatment'* and *'no experience in this area'*. The two exceptions to this were the questions on funding (including charities and public donations) which read: *Does your organisation ever experience unfair treatment because of religion when applying for funding in any of the following areas?* and the questions on the media, which read: *How often, if ever, does your organisation or religious community experience unfair treatment because of their religion in any of the following areas?*

2. The first figure is the number of organisations stating that their members experienced unfair treatment. The figures in brackets show the breakdown of this number between 'frequent' and 'occasional'. The figure after the slash (/) is the total number of organisations answering the question (excluding those who indicated they had no experience in the area). So, for example, the entry 94(8+86)/237 for Christian organisations against school teachers means that 237 Christian organisations answered this question; 8 reported that their members or their children experienced frequent unfair treatment from teachers because of their religion and 86 reported that they experienced occasional unfair treatment, making a total of 94.

3. The number of respondents varies from one question to the next because those who ticked that they had no experience in the area concerned have been excluded from the totals. In addition, some respondents skipped individual questions, or whole sections of the questionnaire. The total number of questionnaires returned by a religious tradition, whether fully completed or not, is given in the first row.

---

13 For the education questions, organisations were asked about 'your members or their children'.

4. Organisations representing Chinese and 'other' religious groups have been excluded because most questions were answered by between one and three respondents.

Part 3

This table gives responses to the question '*Which of the following measures, if any, do you think should be considered in order to combat unfair treatment on the basis of religion?*' Respondents were asked to tick up to three measures and to make their own suggestions if they wished. The table gives the number of respondents who chose each measure on the list: these figures sum to more than the totals at the foot of the table because respondents could choose more than one measure. As explained in chapter 14, some people ticked up to 6, and the average number varied between religions. This makes it more difficult to make direct comparisons between (as opposed to within) religious groups.

Part 1

	Bahá'í 25	Buddhist 33	Christian 311	Hindu 37	Jain 7	Jewish 40
Max respondents						
Schools						
Teachers	2(1+1)/19	3(0+3)/13	94(8+86)/237	14(1+13)/21	1(1+0)/2	7(0+7)/20
Pupils	5(1+4)/19	5(0+5)/15	144(18+126)/242	20(3+17)/24	2(0+2)/4	18(0+18)/22
Policies	4(2+2)/18	3(1+2)/15	53(2+51)/234	7(2+5)/19	1(0+1)/3	5(0+5)/20
Practices	5(2+3)/18	6(1+5)/15	66(5+61)/235	10(2+8)/18	2(0+2)/2	9(0+9)/20
RE curriculum	8(3+5)/19	8(2+6)/20	65(14+51)/241	15(7+8)/24	3(1+2)/5	5(0+5)/22
RE teaching	8(3+5)/19	9(2+7)/19	77(16+61)/238	14(9+5)/21	2(1+1)/4	8(0+8)/22
Citizenship studies	3(1+2)/13	2(1+1)/13	15(3+12)/174	5(1+4)/13	2(1+1)/3	1(0+1)/15
Collective worship	7(1+6)/17	8(3+5)/15	54(5+49)/226	14(5+9)/22	2(1+1)/4	12(2+10)/21
Higher education						
Staff	2(1+1)/14	1(0+1)/16	61(3+58)/146	6(1+5)/18	0/2	7(0+7)/18
Students	4(1+3)/14	2(0+2)/16	60(4+56)/145	13(1+12)/22	0/2	14(2+12)/19
Policies	1(1+1)/14	2(1+1)/17	26(5+21)/134	5(0+5)/16	0/2	4(0+4)/17
Practices	3(1+2)/15	2(1+1)/17	29(5+24)/132	5(0+5)/14	0/2	9(1+8)/20
Local education authorities						
Officials	4(1+3)/17	3(0+3)/13	32(2+30)/171	9(4+5)/20	2(1+1)/3	6(0+6)/19
Policies	4(1+3)/15	4(1+3)/14	43(6+37)/179	7(1+6)/19	2(1+1)/3	7(1+6)/19
Practices	3(1+2)/14	4(1+3)/14	42(6+36)/177	8(1+7)/18	2(1+1)/3	6(1+5)/18
Private sector employers						
Managers	4(1+3)/21	3(1+2)/19	92(11+81)/220	17(7+10)/23	2(1+1)/4	11(0+11)/17
Colleagues	5(1+4)/20	2(1+1)/19	94(6+88)/219	16(2+14)/21	2(1+1)/4	10(0+10)/15
Policies	4(1+3)/18	1(1+0)/16	43(6+37)/193	13(4+9)/19	2(1+1)/4	7(0+7)/14
Practices	5(1+4)/18	2(1+1)/17	47(7+40)/188	13(2+11)/17	2(1+1)/4	8(0+8)/14

	Bahá'í	Buddhist	Christian	Hindu	Jain	Jewish
Public sector employers						
Managers	4(1+3)/18	3(1+2)/18	69(4+65)/204	18(5+13)/22	2(1+1)/2	6(0+6)/16
Colleagues	4(1+3)/18	2(1+1)/18	79(4+75)/205	16(5+11)/22	2(1+1)/2	9(0+9)/17
Policies	3(1+2)/17	2(1+1)/17	33(2+31)/189	12(5+7)/20	2(1+1)/2	4(0+4)/14
Practices	5(2+3)/17	1(1+0)/17	43(5+38)/187	13(4+9)/19	2(1+1)/2	5(0+5)/15
Voluntary sector employers						
Managers	3(1+2)/13	1(1+0)/15	22(3+19)/174	11(1+10)/19	1(0+1)/2	3(0+3)/15
Colleagues	4(1+3)/13	1(1+0)/15	32(3+29)/179	9(0+9)/18	1(0+1)/2	5(0+5)/16
Policies	3(1+2)/13	1(1+0)/14	14(1+13)/168	9(1+8)/17	1(0+1)/2	2(0+2)/15
Practices	4(1+3)/13	1(1+0)/15	18(2+16)/168	10(1+9)/16	1(0+1)/2	1(0+1)/14
Jobcentres						
Staff	1(1+0)/10	0/15	16(1+15)/165	11(2+9)/18	2(1+1)/3	2(0+2)/8
Policies	1(1+0)/10	0/15	8(1+7)/160	9(1+8)/16	2(1+1)/3	3(0+3)/8
Practices	1(1+0)/10	0/15	11(1+10)/162	9(2+7)/14	2(1+1)/3	4(0+4)/9
Private employment agencies						
Staff	1(1+0)/13	1(1+0)/14	16(2+14)/150	9(4+5)/16	2(0+2)/3	2(0+2)/9
Policies	1(1+0)/12	1(1+0)/14	9(1+8)/145	8(2+6)/14	2(0+2)/3	2(0+2)/9
Practices	1(1+0)/12	1(1+0)/14	11(2+9)/145	8(3+5)/14	2(0+2)/3	3(0+3)/9
Owning or buying a house						
Estate agent staff	1(1+0)/18	0/19	11(1+10)/208	9(1+8)/20	2(1+1)/4	2(0+2)/14
Policies/practices	2(1+1)/18	0/19	8(0+8)/201	7(1+6)/19	2(1+1)/4	0/13
Neighbours	3(1+2)/19	1(0+1)/19	40(2+38)/214	16(5+11)/20	1(1+0)/4	6(0+6)/13
Private renting						
Landlords	3(1+2)/14	1(0+1)/18	21(3+18)/202	18(3+15)/25	1(0+1)/2	3(0+3)/14
Policies/practices	3(1+2)/14	0/17	15(1+14)/196	11(2+9)/18	1(0+1)/2	2(0+2)/13
Lettings agents	1(1+0)/12	0/17	10(0+10)/189	14(3+11)/22	1(0+1)/2	1(0+1)/14
Policies/practices	1(1+0)/13	0/17	5(0+5)/183	9(1+8)/18	1(0+1)/2	1(0+1)/14
Other tenants	2(1+1)/14	0/17	23(0+23)/191	14(3+11)/20	1(0+1)/2	6(1+5)/13

Renting from a council						
Council staff	1(1+0)/13	0/16	12(1+11)/198	10(2+8)/21	1(1+0)/2	1(1+0)/11
Policies	1(1+0)/12	0/16	7(2+5)/190	6(0+6)/18	1(1+0)/2	1(1+0)/11
Practices	1(1+0)/12	0/16	8(2+6)/187	8(2+6)/17	1(1+0)/2	1(1+0)/11
Other tenants	2(1+1)/13	0/16	30(0+30)/190	12(2+10)/19	1(1+0)/2	5(0+5)/11
Tenants' associations	1(1+0)/11	0/16	7(0+7)/178	6(1+5)/18	1(1+0)/2	1(0+1)/10
Renting from housing associations						
HA staff	0/11	0/14	11(2+9)/180	8(0+8)/19	1(1+0)/2	1(0+1)/11
Policies	0/11	0/14	5(0+5)/176	6(0+6)/17	1(1+0)/2	0/10
Practices	0/11	0/14	9(1+8)/176	7(0+7)/16	1(1+0)/2	1(0+1)/11
Other tenants	1(0+1)/11	0/14	23(2+21)/177	9(0+9)/19	1(1+0)/2	2(0+2)/10
Tenants' associations	0/11	0/14	6(1+5)/168	6(0+6)/17	1(1+0)/2	1(0+1)/10
Surgeries and health centres						
GPs/medical staff	2(1+1)/23	0/24	41(2+39)/237	10(3+7)/29	2(1+1)/4	1(0+1)/21
Non-medical staff	3(1+2)/23	0/23	28(4+24)/228	11(0+11)/27	3(1+2)/4	0/19
Policies/practices	1(1+0)/23	0/24	23(3+20)/231	6(0+6)/23	1(1+0)/3	1(0+1)/21
NHS hospitals						
Medical staff	1(1+0)/21	0/25	37(5+32)/234	14(2+12)/30	2(1+1)/4	2(0+2)/20
Non-medical staff	2(1+1)/21	0/25	24(2+22)/226	13(2+11)/28	2(1+1)/4	2(0+2)/19
Patients	2(1+1)/20	0/24	26(1+25)/223	10(1+9)/27	2(1+1)/4	2(0+2)/19
Policies	2(1+1)/20	0/24	19(4+15)/217	6(2+4)/23	2(1+1)/4	0/19
Practices	1(1+0)/19	1(0+1)/24	23(4+19)/216	7(2+5)/23	2(1+1)/4	1(0+1)/20
Private health care						
Medical staff	2(1+1)/17	0/18	13(2+11)/177	3(0+3)/19	2(1+1)/3	1(0+1)/20
Non-medical staff	3(1+2)/17	0/18	13(2+11)/176	4(1+3)/19	2(1+1)/3	1(0+1)/20
Patients	3(1+2)/16	0/18	11(1+10)/173	3(1+2)/18	2(1+1)/3	2(0+2)/20
Policies/practices	2(1+1)/17	0/17	9(1+8)/175	4(1+3)/17	2(1+1)/3	0/20
The police service						
Police officers	0/14	1(0+1)/18	35(4+31)/223	23(7+16)/29	1(1+0)/3	6(1+5)/22
Policies	0/14	0/16	13(2+11)/204	11(1+10)/22	1(1+0)/3	0/20
Practices	1(0+1)/14	0/17	26(2+24)/207	17(4+13)/24	1(1+0)/3	3(1+2)/22

	Bahá'í	Buddhist	Christian	Hindu	Jain	Jewish
Legal services						
Lawyers	3(1+2)/16	0/18	15(1+14)/197	8(0+8)/19	1(1+0)/3	2(0+2)/22
Court staff	3(1+2)/10	1(0+1)/15	15(0+15)/177	7(0+7)/17	1(1+0)/3	3(0+3)/19
Policies/practices	3(1+2)/9	0/15	15(0+15)/176	4(1+3)/13	1(1+0)/3	1(0+1)/17
The prison service						
Staff	1(0+1)/5	5(0+5)/13	21(3+18)/125	9(5+4)/14	1(1+0)/2	7(1+6)/11
Inmates	0/3	1(0+1)/10	17(1+16)/116	5(3+2)/9	1(1+0)/2	5(1+4)/10
Policies	0/3	5(1+4)/13	8(1+7)/113	5(3+2)/8	1(1+0)/2	2(1+1)/10
Practices	1(0+1)/4	5(1+4)/12	12(1+11)/116	5(3+2)/7	1(1+0)/2	6(1+5)/11
The probation service						
Staff	0/2	0/7	9(2+7)/119	4(1+3)/8	1(1+0)/2	1(0+1)/10
Policies	0/2	0/6	6(2+4)/114	2(0+2)/6	1(1+0)/2	0/9
Practices	0/2	0/7	6(1+5)/115	2(0+2)/5	1(1+0)/2	0/9
Immigration authorities						
Staff	3(1+2)/13	3(1+2)/14	20(5+15)/108	17(7+10)/24	2(1+1)/4	3(0+3)/10
Policies	4(1+3)/13	1(0+1)/13	15(4+11)/104	11(6+5)/18	2(1+1)/4	1(0+1)/9
Practices	4(1+3)/13	2(0+2)/13	17(4+13)/106	13(6+7)/19	2(1+1)/4	2(0+2)/10
Social services						
Staff	2(1+1)/15	1(1+0)/18	51(12+39)/221	13(1+12)/24	2(1+1)/3	4(0+4)/18
Policies	2(1+1)/15	1(1+0)/18	34(8+26)/206	7(0+7)/18	1(1+0)/3	1(0+1)/18
Practices	3(1+2)/15	1(1+0)/18	42(10+32)/209	8(0+8)/18	2(1+1)/4	4(0+4)/19
The Benefits Agency						
Staff	2(1+1)/16	1(1+0)/20	14(2+12)/199	10(2+8)/20	1(1+0)/3	3(1+2)/13
Policies/practices	2(1+1)/16	1(1+0)/20	10(1+9)/192	6(0+6)/16	1(1+0)/3	3(1+2)/13
Local authority planning services						
Planners	0/10	1(1+0)/20	40(6+34)/194	11(3+8)/19	1(1+0)/3	3(1+2)/16
Policies	0/10	1(1+0)/20	26(3+23)/180	9(3+6)/17	2(1+1)/4	4(1+3)/16
Practices	0/10	1(1+0)/20	37(8+29)/184	10(2+8)/17	1(1+0)/3	5(1+4)/16

Local authority leisure services						
Staff	1(1+0)/18	1(1+0)/19	11(0+11)/201	9(1+8)/24	1(1+0)/2	3(0+3)/13
Policies	1(1+0)/17	1(1+0)/18	6(0+6)/193	5(0+5)/20	1(1+0)/2	0/13
Practices	1(1+0)/18	1(1+0)/18	8(0+8)/194	6(0+6)/19	1(1+0)/2	2(0+2)/13
Public transport						
Staff	1(1+0)/18	1(1+0)/22	9(0+9)/215	10(0+10)/23	1(1+0)/3	4(1+3)/17
Policies/practices	1(1+0)/17	1(1+0)/21	11(1+10)/203	7(0+7)/19	1(1+0)/3	2(0+2)/16
Shops and stores						
Staff	2(1+1)/20	2(1+1)/24	21(1+20)/229	9(1+8)/24	2(0+2)/4	5(0+5)/22
Customers	2(1+1)/20	1(1+0)/24	18(1+17)/222	11(2+9)/22	2(0+2)/4	7(0+7)/22
Policies/practices	1(1+0)/19	2(1+1)/24	16(5+11)/218	7(1+6)/21	2(0+2)/4	3(1+2)/21
Charities and trusts						
Staff	2(1+1)/8	3(1+2)/17	25(4+21)/192	8(2+6)/18	1(1+0)/2	2(1+1)/22
Policies	2(1+1)/8	4(1+3)/16	40(10+30)/190	10(5+5)/17	1(1+0)/2	2(2+0)/22
Practices	2(1+1)/8	4(1+3)/16	38(8+30)/185	10(4+6)/17	1(1+0)/2	1(1+0)/22
Local government funding						
Staff	2(1+1)/6	4(1+3)/17	39(9+30)/170	12(4+8)/23	1(0+1)/2	4(1+3)/20
Policies	1(1+0)/6	3(1+2)/16	45(8+37)/162	10(5+5)/19	1(0+1)/2	3(2+1)/20
Practices	1(1+0)/6	4(1+3)/16	48(9+39)/164	15(6+9)/23	1(0+1)/2	6(1+5)/20
Central government funding						
Staff	1(1+0)/6	4(1+3)/14	26(7+19)/128	10(3+7)/17	1(0+1)/2	3(1+2)/19
Policies	1(1+0)/6	7(1+6)/15	40(10+30)/133	10(5+5)/15	1(0+1)/2	2(1+1)/19
Practices	1(1+0)/5	6(1+5)/14	39(9+30)/129	11(4+7)/16	1(0+1)/2	3(1+2)/19
Public donation						
General public	0/3	4(1+3)/19	39(6+33)/184	10(5+5)/19	1(0+1)/2	2(1+1)/19
National newspapers/magazines						
Journalists	6(3+3)/17	15(1+14)/26	171(45+126)/243	19(8+11)/25	2(2+0)/4	18(5+13)/30
Coverage of org.	5(4+1)/17	10(1+9)/25	127(31+96)/221	17(9+8)/24	3(2+1)/4	6(1+5)/24
Coverage of religion	6(3+3)/17	13(2+11)/25	186(56+130)/260	16(8+8)/24	3(2+1)/4	19(3+16)/30

	Bahá'í	Buddhist	Christian	Hindu	Jain	Jewish
Local newspapers/magazines						
Journalists	11(2+9)/22	6(1+5)/25	122(19+103)/245	16(6+10)/25	2(2+0)/4	11(2+9)/28
Coverage of org.	9(4+5)/21	3(1+2)/23	97(19+78)/226	15(8+7)/23	3(2+1)/4	5(1+4)/25
Coverage of religion	11(4+7)/22	6(1+5)/25	124(27+97)/245	16(8+8)/25	3(2+1)/4	13(2+11)/30
National radio						
Journalists	4(1+3)/16	7(1+6)/25	144(35+109)/221	16(8+8)/24	3(2+1)/4	11(4+7)/27
Coverage of org.	5(3+2)/17	5(1+4)/25	100(24+76)/188	15(8+7)/23	3(3+0)/4	4(1+3)/22
Coverage of religion	5(3+2)/17	7(2+5)/26	146(40+106)/227	16(7+9)/23	3(3+0)/4	16(4+12)/29
Local radio						
Journalists	7(1+6)/21	5(1+4)/24	95(13+82)/219	15(6+9)/24	3(2+1)/4	8(3+5)/24
Coverage of org.	6(3+3)/20	3(1+2)/23	70(9+61)/197	13(6+7)/24	3(3+0)/4	2(1+1)/22
Coverage of religion	7(3+4)/21	5(1+4)/23	90(17+73)/214	13(6+7)/25	3(3+0)/4	11(3+8)/25
Television						
Journalists	5(3+2)/15	10(1+9)/26	158(45+113)/226	18(9+9)/25	3(2+1)/4	13(5+8)/28
Coverage of org.	6(4+2)/14	5(1+4)/22	113(31+82)/190	18(9+9)/25	3(3+0)/4	4(1+3)/18
Coverage of religion	6(4+2)/15	10(2+8)/26	176(56+120)/238	17(8+9)/24	3(3+0)/4	18(5+13)/30

	Muslim	NRM/Pagan	Sikh	Zoroastrian	Inter-faith
Max respondents	70	27	35	7	27
Schools					
Teachers	44(15+29)/50	14(5+9)/18	23(8+15)/30	3(0+3)/5	6(1+5)/13
Pupils	41(16+25)/49	13(2+11)/16	28(12+16)/31	4(0+4)/5	11(2+9)/13
Policies	35(16+19)/50	13(7+6)/17	17(6+11)/26	1(0+1)/5	4(1+3)/12
Practices	38(13+25)/51	14(6+8)/17	18(6+12)/27	1(0+1)/5	6(1+5)/12
RE curriculum	42(20+22)/54	16(13+3)/18	21(8+13)/29	2(2+0)/3	6(2+4)/17
RE teaching	42(21+21)/53	14(11+3)/16	19(9+10)/30	2(2+0)/3	4(1+3)/14
Citizenship studies	19(7+12)/36	4(1+3)/8	6(1+5)/15	2(1+1)/5	1(0+1)/6
Collective worship	37(18+19)/47	10(8+2)/13	18(4+14)/27	2(2+0)/5	8(1+7)/13

Higher education					
Staff	32(10+22)/45	9(2+7)/18	14(2+12)/23	2(1+1)/5	5(0+5)/12
Students	31(10+21)/44	11(0+11)/17	18(3+15)/27	3(1+2)/5	8(0+8)/12
Policies	27(12+15)/42	7(2+5)/17	11(2+9)/26	3(1+2)/5	2(0+2)/10
Practices	33(12+21)/44	7(2+5)/15	16(2+14)/25	3(1+2)/5	6(0+6)/11
Local education authorities					
Officials	37(16+21)/49	10(6+4)/15	16(3+13)/26	2(1+1)/5	5(0+5)/12
Policies	34(15+19)/49	9(8+1)/15	14(2+12)/24	3(1+2)/5	3(0+3)/11
Practices	38(17+21)/48	9(8+1)/15	17(2+15)/25	3(1+2)/5	6(0+6)/13
Private sector employers					
Managers	46(25+21)/55	11(2+9)/15	26(7+19)/30	4(1+3)/5	1(1+6)/9
Colleagues	49(15+34)/55	13(2+11)/17	23(6+17)/29	4(0+4)/5	6(2+4)/8
Policies	37(20+17)/48	6(2+4)/14	27(2+25)/31	4(0+4)/5	6(0+6)/8
Practices	41(20+21)/49	8(3+5)/14	26(4+22)/30	4(1+3)/5	6(1+5)/8
Public sector employers					
Managers	39(19+20)/47	13(4+9)/16	24(6+18)/31	3(1+2)/5	6(1+5)/9
Colleagues	37(13+24)/47	12(2+10)/16	23(5+18)/30	4(0+4)/5	6(1+5)/9
Policies	34(19+15)/47	9(2+7)/14	18(3+15)/28	3(0+3)/5	4(0+4)/8
Practices	41(19+22)/50	11(3+8)/15	24(5+19)/30	3(0+3)/5	6(1+5)/9
Voluntary sector employers					
Managers	26(8+18)/44	7(1+6)/12	13(1+12)/22	2(1+1)/5	6(0+6)/8
Colleagues	28(5+23)/47	8(1+7)/13	11(1+10)/20	2(1+1)/5	6(0+6)/8
Policies	24(7+17)/42	7(3+4)/11	12(1+11)/21	2(0+2)/5	3(0+3)/8
Practices	29(7+22)/44	7(2+5)/11	12(1+11)/21	2(0+2)/5	4(0+4)/8
Jobcentres					
Staff	32(15+17)/47	5(5+0)/9	10(2+8)/19	3(1+2)/5	3(0+3)/4
Policies	28(12+16)/48	5(5+0)/9	12(2+10)/21	3(1+2)/5	2(0+2)/4
Practices	31(13+18)/47	5(5+0)/9	11(2+9)/20	3(1+2)/5	2(0+2)/4

	Muslim	NRM/Pagan	Sikh	Zoroastrian	Inter-faith
Private employment agencies					
Staff	36(14+22)/47	4(3+1)/8	13(4+9)21	3(0+3)/5	3(0+3)/4
Policies	33(15+18)/47	4(1+3)/8	10(4+6)/20	3(0+3)/5	2(0+2)/3
Practices	35(16+19)/47	2(1+1)/7	12(3+9)/18	3(0+3)/5	3(0+3)/4
Owning or buying a house					
Estate agent staff	23(11+12)/46	2(0+2)/13	13(3+10)/24	3(2+1)/5	3(0+3)/6
Policies/practices	24(8+16)/44	2(0+2)/13	9(2+7)/19	3(1+2)/5	2(0+2)/4
Neighbours	36(5+31)/46	9(2+7)/16	24(4+20)/29	4(2+2)/5	6(2+4)/8
Private renting					
Landlords	31(12+19)/42	10(1+9)/15	17(2+15)/19	2(2+0)/4	4(0+4)/6
Policies/practices	30(8+22)/41	6(1+5)/15	17(3+14)/19	2(2+0)/4	3(0+3)/5
Lettings agents	25(9+6)/38	3(1+2)/12	16(2+14)/19	2(1+1)/4	4(0+4)/6
Policies/practices	24(9+15)/37	2(1+1)/12	13(2+11)/18	2(1+1)/4	2(0+2)/5
Other tenants	32(12+20)/40	12(2+10)/16	19(3+16)/22	2(2+0)/4	4(1+3)/6
Renting from a council					
Council staff	34(13+21)/45	7(2+5)/12	13(4+9)/24	2(1+1)/4	4(1+3)/6
Policies	28(9+19)/44	5(1+4)/12	9(1+8)/20	2(1+1)/4	0/4
Practices	32(11+21)/46	6(2+4)/12	13(3+10)/23	2(1+1)/4	2(1+1)/5
Other tenants	37(15+22)/46	5(2+3)/11	20(4+16)/23	3(1+2)/4	4(2+2)/6
Tenants' associations	26(8+18)/39	2(1+1)/10	11(2+9)/18	2(1+1)/4	2(0+2)/4
Renting from housing associations					
HA staff	27(6+21)/38	2(0+2)/7	11(1+10)/17	1(1+0)/3	2(0+2)/4
Policies	25(6+19)/38	2(0+2)/7	7(1+6)/13	1(1+0)/3	1(0+1)/4
Practices	29(7+22)/39	1(0+1)/7	7(2+5)/13	1(1+0)/3	1(0+1)/4
Other tenants	29(10+19)/37	1(1+0)/6	12(2+10)/14	1(1+0)/3	3(1+2)/5
Tenants' associations	26(6+20)/35	1(0+1)/6	2(2+5)/10	1(1+0)/3	2(0+2)/4

Surgeries and health centres

GPs/medical staff	23(5+18)/50	7(2+5)/16	19(1+18)/30	3(0+3)/4	4(0+4)/11
Non-medical staff	28(8+20)/50	6(3+3)/16	20(2+18)/31	3(0+3)/4	3(0+3)/9
Policies/practices	20(8+12)/48	6(1+5)/15	15(1+14)/28	2(0+2)/5	2(0+2)/10

NHS hospitals

Medical staff	28(10+18)/53	9(1+8)/17	22(3+19)/34	3(0+3)/5	5(0+5)/10
Non-medical staff	31(10+21)/53	9(1+8)/16	21(4+17)/33	3(0+3)/5	7(1+6)/11
Patients	22(7+15)/49	4(1+3)/14	16(2+14)/28	2(0+2)/4	5(0+5)/10
Policies	20(9+11)/47	8(1+7)/14	9(0+9)/25	2(0+2)/4	3(2+1)/11
Practices	24(9+15)/46	8(1+7)/14	12(2+10)/24	2(0+2)/4	7(1+6)/11

Private health care

Medical staff	15(2+13)/34	1(0+1)/5	9(1+8)/21	1(0+1)/3	1(0+1)/6
Non-medical staff	14(2+12)/34	1(0+1)/4	8(1+7)/21	1(0+1)/3	1(0+1)/6
Patients	16(4+12)/34	1(0+1)/4	7(1+6)/18	1(0+1)/3	2(0+2)/7
Policies/practices	14(3+11)/34	1(1+0)/4	7(1+6)/20	1(0+1)/3	1(0+1)/6

The police service

Police officers	44(21+23)/54	11(3+8)/16	28(8+20)/32	4(1+3)/6	6(3+3)/10
Policies	36(15+21)/53	10(2+8)/16	16(4+12)/26	3(1+2)/6	2(2+0)/9
Practices	42(21+21)/54	10(2+8)/16	24(7+17)/26	3(1+2)/6	4(2+2)/8

Legal services

Lawyers	25(7+18)/45	4(1+3)/12	11(1+10)/22	3(2+1)/6	3(1+2)/9
Court staff	23(8+15)/42	6(1+5)/11	12(2+10)/20	3(2+1)/6	3(1+2)/9
Policies/practices	21(7+14)/41	6(2+4)/12	9(1+8)/19	3(2+1)/6	2(0+2)/9

The prison service

Prison staff	34(15+19)/38	10(2+8)/12	14(5+9)/16	1(1+0)/2	4(2+2)/6
Inmates	31(16+15)/37	7(0+7)/10	12(1+11)/14	1(1+0)/2	4(2+2)/6
Policies	25(11+14)/39	8(4+4)/12	11(3+8)/15	1(1+0)/2	3(1+2)/6
Practices	28(13+15)/39	10(4+6)/12	13(2+11)/15	1(1+0)/2	4(2+2)/6

	Muslim	NRM/Pagan	Sikh	Zoroastrian	Inter-faith
The probation service					
Staff	21(9+12)/29	4(2+2)/6	6(0+6)/8	1(1+0)/2	2(1+1)/7
Policies	19(8+11)/30	2(1+1)/4	4(0+4)/8	1(1+0)/2	1(1+0)/6
Practices	22(8+14)/30	4(2+2)/6	4(0+4)/8	1(1+0)/2	2(1+1)/6
Immigration authorities					
Staff	39(21+18)/47	3(2+1)/5	24(7+17)/30	5(1+4)/6	5(3+2)/8
Policies	38(21+17)/48	3(3+0)/5	20(6+14)/31	4(1+3)/5	4(3+1)/6
Practices	38(21+17)/48	3(3+0)/5	20(5+15)/29	5(1+4)/6	5(3+2)/7
Social services					
Staff	39(10+29)/50	11(5+6)/15	16(1+15)/26	2(0+2)/3	3(0+3)/8
Policies	29(7+22)/47	8(4+4)/13	10(1+9)/24	2(0+2)/3	0/6
Practices	37(8+29)/49	11(5+6)/15	15(2+13)/24	3(0+3)/4	2(0+2)/6
The Benefits Agency					
Staff	22(3+19)/44	5(1+4)/12	12(2+10)/25	4(1+3)/4	3(1+2)/6
Policies/practices	20(4+16)/45	5(1+4)/12	9(1+8)/21	2(0+2)/3	2(0+2)/6
Local authority planning services					
Planners	36(17+19)/45	4(2+2)/8	11(1+10)/22	2(0+2)/4	3(0+3)/7
Policies	30(15+15)/45	3(2+1)/7	7(1+6)/19	2(0+2)/4	1(0+1)/6
Practices	33(14+19)/44	3(2+1)/7	9(2+7)/21	2(0+2)/4	0/6
Local authority leisure services					
Staff	27(13+14)/42	3(0+3)/10	8(0+8)/24	2(0+2)/4	1(0+1)/5
Policies	25(12+13)/41	2(1+1)/10	8(2+6)/25	2(0+2)/4	3(0+3)/6
Practices	24(11+13)/41	3(0+3)/11	9(1+8)/25	2(0+2)/4	3(0+3)/5
Public transport					
Staff	18(6+12)/47	1(0+1)/13	9(1+8)/26	1(0+1)/4	2(0+2)/6
Policies/practices	12(2+10)/47	0/12	5(1+4)/26	2(1+1)/4	0/5

Shops and stores					
Staff	21(4+17)/50	4(1+3)/14	12(2+10)/25	2(0+2)/5	3(0+3)/7
Customers	19(4+15)/49	3(1+2)/13	10(1+9)/24	1(0+1)/4	3(0+3)/7
Policies/practices	21(4+17)/50	2(0+2)/13	7(2+5)/25	1(0+1)/4	2(0+2)/6
Charities and trusts					
Staff	20(10+10)/38	5(4+1)/7	7(2+5)/19	2(0+2)/4	4(1+3)/11
Policies	18(12+6)/37	4(3+1)/5	7(2+5)/19	2(0+2)/4	4(2+2)/11
Practices	19(11+8)/36	3(3+0)/5	5(1+4)/17	2(0+2)/4	4(2+2)/11
Local government funding					
Staff	29(15+14)/43	3(2+1)/6	13(4+9)/23	3(1+2)/5	5(4+1)/11
Policies	29(18+11)/45	3(3+0)/6	11(3+8)/21	3(1+2)/5	4(3+1)/10
Practices	32(19+13)/46	3(3+0)/6	12(3+9)/21	3(1+2)/5	4(3+1)/10
Central government funding					
Staff	24(14+10)/35	4(4+0)/5	9(4+5)/14	2(0+2)/3	3(1+2)/6
Policies	22(14+8)/33	5(5+0)/6	7(3+4)/13	2(0+2)/3	2(0+2)/5
Practices	24(13+11)/35	5(5+0)/6	8(3+5)/13	2(0+2)/3	2(0+2)/5
Public donation					
General public	19(4+15)/32	2(1+1)/8	10(1+9)/18	1(0+1)/4	3(1+2)/8
National newspapers/magazines					
Journalists	48(38+10)/53	17(9+8)/22	24(8+16)/28	2(1+1)/5	7(6+1)/14
Coverage of org.	29(16+13)/37	8(6+2)/20	18(4+14)/24	2(1+1)/4	5(4+1)/13
Coverage of religion	50(44+6)/55	18(10+8)/21	28(7+21)/30	3(1+2)/5	10(6+4)/14
Local newspapers/magazines					
Journalists	43(24+19)/50	15(8+7)/22	19(3+16)/29	2(1+1)/4	6(2+4)/17
Coverage of org.	26(14+12)/40	11(6+5)/19	12(6+6)/25	2(1+1)/4	5(3+2)/18
Coverage of religion	47(28+19)/53	17(9+8)/20	20(7+13)/28	2(2+0)/4	5(3+2)/17

	Muslim	NRM/Pagan	Sikh	Zoroastrian	Inter-faith
National radio					
Journalists	44(20+44)/52	12(6+6)/19	16(2+14)/23	2(1+1)/5	6(2+4)/14
Coverage of org.	26(10+16)/39	8(3+5)/16	8(2+6)/18	2(1+1)/5	3(2+1)/12
Coverage of religion	48(28+20)/55	16(8+8)/21	12(2+10)/20	3(2+1)/6	7(3+4)/14
Local radio					
Journalists	39(17+22)/46	11(3+8)/16	12(3+9)/23	1(1+0)/3	7(1+6)/16
Coverage of org.	24(13+11)/37	7(1+6)/14	6(2+4)/19	1(1+0)/3	4(1+3)/17
Coverage of religion	41(23+18)/47	12(5+7)/17	15(5+10)/24	2(2+0)/4	5(1+4)/15
Television					
Journalists	45(27+18)/50	16(7+9)/21	20(9+11)/27	2(1+1)/5	7(3+4)/13
Coverage of org.	24(13+11)/31	8(3+5)/16	10(3+7)/20	2(1+1)/5	6(2+4)/14
Coverage of religion	47(31+16)/52	18(8+10)/21	18(8+10)/25	3(2+1)/6	9(3+6)/15

Part 2

	Anglican	Baptist	Black Led	Methodist	New Church	Orthodox
Max respondents	27	24	15	27	21	9
Schools						
Teachers	4(0+4)/21	8(1+7)/22	10(1+9)/11	6(0+6)/18	8(0+8)/19	1(1+0)/7
Pupils	14(2+12)/23	13(1+12)/24	6(2+4)/7	7(2+5)/18	9(0+9)/19	2(0+2)/5
Policies	1(0+1)/21	2(0+2)/23	4(1+3)/8	5(0+5)/18	4(0+4)/18	2(0+2)/6
Practices	4(0+4)/22	2(1+1)/22	4(1+3)/8	4(0+4)/18	5(0+5)/19	1(0+1)/6
RE curriculum	6(0+6)/22	2(1+1)/22	6(2+4)/8	3(0+3)/19	4(0+4)/16	2(0+2)/7
RE teaching	4(0+4)/22	4(2+2)/21	5(1+4)/7	4(1+3)/18	4(0+4)/16	2(0+2)/7
Citizenship studies	1(0+1)/19	0/11	3(1+2)/8	0/13	0/11	0/6
Collective worship	4(0+4)/23	2(0+2)/20	4(0+4)/9	5(0+5)/18	1(0+1)/15	2(0+2)/6

Higher education						
Staff	1(0+1)/6	3(0+3)/9	6(1+5)/8	4(0+4)/8	3(0+3)/8	1(0+1)/6
Students	2(0+2)/7	3(0+3)/9	5(1+4)/7	2(0+2)/8	3(0+3)/8	0/5
Policies	0/5	2(0+2)/10	5(1+4)/8	2(0+2)/7	1(0+1)/7	1(0+1)/5
Practices	0/5	1(0+1)/9	4(1+3)/8	2(0+2)/7	1(0+1)/7	1(0+1)/5
Local education authorities						
Officials	3(0+3)/15	2(0+2)/12	5(0+5)/8	3(0+3)/12	1(0+1)/9	1(0+1)/5
Policies	4(0+4)/13	2(0+2)/12	5(1+4)/7	4(0+4)/13	2(0+2)/10	0/4
Practices	5(0+5)/13	1(0+1)/12	5(0+5)/7	4(0+4)/13	1(0+1)/10	0/4
Private sector employers						
Private managers	8(0+8)/15	8(0+8)/18	9(3+6)/11	7(0+7)/19	6(0+6)/17	1(0+1)/7
Private colleagues	7(0+7)/16	6(0+6)/18	5(1+4)/7	7(0+7)/17	10(1+9)/19	1(0+1)/7
Private policies	2(0+2)/10	5(0+5)/16	5(0+5)/8	4(1+3)/15	2(0+2)/12	1(0+1)/7
Private practices	3(0+3)/10	6(0+6)/16	5(0+5)/8	4(1+3)/14	2(0+2)/12	2(0+2)/7
Public sector employers						
Managers	4(0+4)/13	4(0+4)/15	8(1+7)/10	4(0+4)/18	4(0+4)/16	2(0+2)7
Colleagues	3(0+3)/12	6(0+6)/15	10(1+9)/12	6(0+6)/17	5(0+5)/17	0/6
Policies	1(0+1)/10	3(0+3)/15	6(0+6)/8	3(0+3)/16	3(0+3)/14	0/6
Practices	2(1+1)/10	4(0+4)/15	5(1+4)/7	1(0+1)/14	4(0+4)/14	1(0+1)/6
Voluntary sector employers						
Managers	0/9	1(0+1)/13	4(1+3)/7	2(0+2)/17	0/10	1(0+1)/5
Colleagues	0/9	1(0+1)/13	6(1+5)/9	2(0+2)/16	2(0+2)/12	0/5
Policies	0/8	1(0+1)/13	3(0+3)/6	1(0+1)/15	1(0+1)/11	0/5
Practices	0/9	1(0+1)/13	4(1+3)/7	1(0+1)/16	1(0+1)/11	0/5
Jobcentres						
Staff	0/8	0/10	5(1+4)/9	2(0+2)/16	0/13	0/7
Policies	0/9	1(0+1)/11	2(0+2)/7	1(0+1)/15	0/13	0/7
Practices	0/9	2(0+2)/11	3(0+3)/8	1(0+1)/15	0/13	0/7

	Anglican	Baptist	Black Led	Methodist	New Church	Orthodox
Private employment agencies						
Staff	0/9	0/8	4(1+3)/9	2(0+2)/14	1(0+1)/12	0/7
Policies	0/9	0/8	4(0+4)/8	1(0+1)/12	0/11	0/7
Practices	0/9	0/8	4(1+3)/8	1(0+1)/12	0/11	0/7
Owning or buying a house						
Estate agent staff	0/9	0/20	4(1+3)/9	1(0+1)/20	0/15	1(0+1)/8
Policies/practices	0/8	0/20	4(0+4)/9	1(0+1)/19	0/15	0/7
Neighbours	0/8	2(0+2)/20	6(1+5)/9	1(0+1)/19	2(0+2)/15	1(1+0)/8
Private renting						
Landlords	0/9	0/19	5(2+3)/9	1(0+1)/16	1(0+1)/15	2(0+2)/6
Policies/practices	0/9	0/19	4(0+4)/7	1(0+1)/15	1(0+1)/15	1(0+1)/6
Lettings agents	0/9	0/19	4(0+4)/8	1(0+1)/15	0/13	1(0+1)/6
Policies/practices	0/9	0/18	3(0+3)/6	1(0+1)/15	0/13	0/6
Other tenants	0/8	0/18	5(0+5)/8	1(0+1)/15	1(0+1)/15	0/6
Renting from a council						
Council staff	0/10	0/19	2(1+1)/8	1(0+1)/20	1(0+1)/14	2(0+2)/7
Policies	0/10	0/18	3(1+2)/9	1(0+1)/17	1(0+1)/14	0/6
Practices	0/10	0/18	3(1+2)/8	1(0+1)/17	1(0+1)/13	0/6
Other tenants	1(0+1)/10	1(0+1)/18	5(0+5)/8	1(0+1)/17	3(0+3)/15	0/5
Tenants' associations	0/10	0/17	3(0+3)/9	1(0+1)/17	0/13	0/5
Renting from housing associations						
HA staff	1(0+1)/11	0/18	2(1+1)/6	1(0+1)/20	1(0+1)/13	3(1+2)/6
Policies	0/9	0/18	3(0+3)/7	1(0+1)/18	0/12	0/5
Practices	1(0+1)/11	0/18	3(1+2)/7	1(0+1)/18	0/12	1(0+1)/5
Other tenants	2(2+0)/11	0/18	5(0+5)/8	1(0+1)/17	3(0+3)/14	1(0+1)/5
Tenants' associations	0/9	0/18	3(1+2)/8	1(0+1)/16	0/12	0/5

Surgeries and health centres

GPs/medical staff	0/17	1(0+1)/21	4(0+4)/7	2(0+2)/22	2(0+2)/9
Non-medical staff	0/17	0/21	4(1+3)/7	1(0+1)/20	1(0+1)/8
Policies/practices	0/17	0/21	3(1+2)/6	1(0+1)/20	1(0+1)/8
NHS Hospitals					
Medical staff	1(0+1)/16	1(0+1)/20	3(1+2)/7	2(0+2)/22	2(1+1)/9
Non-medical staff	1(0+1)/16	1(0+1)/20	3(0+3)/7	1(0+1)/20	1(0+1)/8
Patients	0/16	0/20	4(0+4)/7	2(0+2)/20	1(0+1)/7
Policies	1(0+1)/17	0/19	4(2+2)/7	3(0+3)/20	1(0+1)/7
Practices	1(0+1)/17	0/19	4(1+3)/7	3(0+3)/20	2(0+2)/7
Private health care					
Medical staff	0/13	0/15	3(1+2)/5	1(0+1)/18	1(0+1)/7
Non-medical staff	0/13	0/15	3(1+2)/5	1(0+1)/16	2(0+2)/7
Patients	0/13	0/15	4(0+4)/5	1(0+1)/15	1(0+1)/6
Policies/practices	0/13	0/15	3(0+3)/5	1(0+1)/16	2(0+2)/7
The police service					
Police officers	0/18	0/20	7(2+5)/9	2(0+2)/21	1(1+0)/7
Policies	0/18	0/19	4(1+3)/7	1(0+1)/19	0/5
Practices	0/18	1(0+1)/19	6(1+5)/8	1(0+1)/19	0/5
Legal services					
Lawyers	0/11	0/17	3(0+3)/8	0/20	1(1+0)/7
Court staff	0/12	0/16	3(0+3)/7	1(0+1)/18	1(0+1)/4
Policies/practices	0/12	0/16	2(0+2)/6	1(0+1)/18	1(0+1)/4
The prison service					
Prison staff	1(0+1)/8	1(1+0)/9	3(1+2)/5	4(1+3)/15	1(1+0)/3
Inmates	1(0+1)/8	1(0+1)/9	2(0+2)/3	3(1+2)/14	0/2
Policies	0/7	0/9	3(1+2)/4	2(0+2)/14	0/2
Practices	1(0+1)/8	1(0+1)/9	4(1+3)/5	2(0+2)/14	0/2

	Anglican	Baptist	Black Led	Methodist	New Church	Orthodox
The probation service						
Staff	0/8	0/12	2(0+2)/5	1(0+1)/15	0/3	1(1+0)/3
Policies	0/8	0/12	3(1+2)/5	1(0+1)/14	0/3	0/2
Practices	0/8	0/12	2(0+2)/5	1(0+1)/14	0/3	0/2
Immigration authorities						
Staff	0/5	0/6	4(1+3)/6	1(0+1)/12	2(0+2)/4	2(1+1)/6
Policies	0/5	0/6	4(1+3)/6	1(0+1)/10	1(0+1)/4	0/4
Practices	0/5	0/6	5(0+5)/7	1(0+1)/10	1(0+1)/4	1(1+0)/6
Social services						
Staff	1(0+1)/16	1(0+1)/20	6(2+4)/9	3(0+3)/20	2(0+2)/15	3(1+2)/8
Policies	1(0+1)/14	1(0+1)/20	5(1+4)/8	3(0+3)/18	1(0+1)/14	1(0+1)/7
Practices	1(0+1)/16	2(0+2)/20	6(1+5)/8	3(0+3)/18	2(0+2)/15	2(0+2)/7
The Benefits Agency						
Staff	0/13	0/20	3(0+3)/9	1(0+1)/17	1(0+1)/14	2(1+1)/8
Policies/practices	0/13	0/20	2(0+2)/6	1(0+1)/16	1(0+1)/14	1(0+1)/7
Local authority planning services						
Planners	1(0+1)/11	1(0+1)/17	5(1+4)/8	2(0+2)/19	3(0+3)/15	1(0+1)/5
Policies	1(0+1)/10	0/16	4(1+3)/6	2(0+2)/17	2(0+2)/13	1(0+1)/5
Practices	1(0+1)/10	1(0+1)/17	4(1+3)/6	3(0+3)/17	2(0+2)/14	1(0+1)/5
Local authority leisure services						
Staff	0/15	0/19	3(0+3)/7	1(0+1)/20	1(0+1)/14	0/6
Policies	0/15	0/19	3(0+3)/6	1(0+1)/18	1(0+1)/14	0/6
Practices	0/15	0/19	3(0+3)/6	1(0+1)/18	1(0+1)/14	0/6
Public transport						
Staff	0/16	0/21	2(0+2)/8	2(0+2)/21	0/13	1(0+1)/8
Policies/practices	0/16	0/20	2(0+2)/6	2(0+2)/18	0/13	0/7
Shops and stores						
Staff	2(0+2)18	1(0+1)/21	5(1+4)/9	3(0+3)/21	1(0+1)/17	1(0+1)/8
Customers	1(0+1)/18	1(0+1)/21	5(0+5)/8	2(0+2)/19	0/16	0/8
Policies/practices	0/18	0/21	2(0+2)/6	4(1+3)/19	0/16	0/8

Charities and trusts						
Staff	2(0+2)/22	1(0+1)/17	5(2+3)/10	1(0+1)/20	0/9	1(0+1)/5
Policies	3(0+3)/22	4(1+3)/17	6(1+5)/10	5(1+4)/19	0/9	0/4
Practices	4(0+4)/22	4(1+3)/17	4(1+3)/8	5(0+5)/19	0/9	0/4
Local government funding						
Staff	6(0+6)/21	2(0+2)/15	7(2+5)/9	1(0+1)/20	2(2+0)/8	2(0+2)/4
Policies	8(0+8)/22	4(1+3)/15	5(1+4)/7	5(0+5)/19	2(1+1)/7	1(0+1)/4
Practices	8(0+8)/22	3(1+2)/15	5(2+3)/7	5(0+5)/19	2(1+1)/7	2(0+2)/4
Central government funding						
Staff	1(0+1)/18	0/8	6(2+4)/8	1(0+1)/15	1(1+0)/5	2(0+2)/4
Policies	3(0+3)/19	5(1+4)/9	5(1+4)/8	5(0+5)/13	1(0+1)/5	1(0+1)/4
Practices	4(0+4)/19	4(0+4)/9	5(2+3)/8	3(0+3)/12	1(0+1)/5	2(0+2)/4
Public donation						
General public	5(0+5)/21	2(0+2)/16	5(2+3)/7	3(0+3)/21	1(1+0)/9	1(0+1)/5
National newspapers/magazines						
Journalists	12(3+9)/22	11(0+11)/19	10(2+8)/13	10(3+7)/18	10(3+7)/16	6(1+5)/8
Coverage of org.	11(3+8)/22	10(0+10)/21	6(4+2)/9	6(1+5)/18	4(0+4)/10	2(0+2)/5
Coverage of religion	14(3+11)/22	15(3+12)/22	9(3+6)/11	10(4+6)/21	11(4+7)/18	5(2+3)/7
Local newspapers/magazines						
Journalists	7(2+5)/20	8(0+8)/20	6(0+6)/9	6(0+6)/22	5(1+4)18	3(0+3)/7
Coverage of org.	7(2+5)/20	6(0+6)/18	6(2+4)/9	4(0+4)/19	3(0+3)/15	3(0+3)/7
Coverage of religion	7(2+5)/20	9(1+8)/20	8(1+7)/11	6(1+5)/22	6(3+3)/18	3(1+2)/7
National radio						
Journalists	11(2+9)/19	12(2+10)/16	8(4+4)/11	10(1+9)/17	8(2+6)/15	4(1+3)/7
Coverage of org.	7(2+5)/18	8(1+7)/15	6(3+3)/9	7(1+6)/15	2(1+1)/11	1(0+1)/6
Coverage of religion	11(3+8)/21	13(2+11)/18	7(3+4)/10	11(3+8)/18	9(3+6)/16	4(2+2)/8
Local radio						
Journalists	5(1+4)/17	6(0+6)/16	6(2+4)/9	6(1+5)/19	4(2+2)/15	2(0+2)/6
Coverage of org.	3(1+2)/17	5(0+5)/16	3(1+2)/6	3(0+3)/16	2(1+1)/13	1(0+1)/7
Coverage of religion	6(2+4)/19	6(0+6)/17	3(1+2)/7	7(2+5)/19	4(2+2)/15	2(0+2)/7

189

	Anglican	Baptist	Black Led	Methodist	New Church	Orthodox
Television						
Journalists	13(2+11)/18	12(1+11)/15	8(3+5)/11	11(3+8)/18	10(3+7)/14	4(1+3)/8
Coverage of org.	10(4+6)/17	8(0+8)/13	5(2+3)/8	9(2+7)/15	3(2+1)/7	1(0+1)/6
Coverage of religion	15(5+10)/21	14(1+13)/17	7(2+5)/11	13(5+8)/18	12(5+7)/15	4(1+3)/8
	Pentecostal	Presbyterian	Roman Catholic	Independent	Ecumenical	Other
Max respondents	23	6	20	25	27	54
Schools						
Teachers	7(0+7)/18	2(0+2)/6	5(0+5)/15	12(1+11)/24	1(0+1)/19	22(2+20)/38
Pupils	16(1+15)/21	2(0+2)/6	6(0+6)/15	21(3+18)/24	10(1+9)/21	26(3+23)/40
Policies	6(0+6)/16	1(0+1)/6	3(0+3)/15	7(0+7)/25	2(0+2)/21	9(1+8)/37
Practices	8(1+7)/15	1(0+1)/6	3(0+3)/15	8(0+8)/23	5(1+4)/22	12(1+11)/40
RE curriculum	8(1+7)/18	1(0+1)/6	2(0+2)/16	7(1+6)/25	5(2+3)/22	14(5+9)/38
RE teaching	9(1+8)/16	0/6	2(0+2)/16	10(1+9)/25	5(3+2)/20	20(5+15)/41
Citizenship studies	3(0+3)/10	2(1+1)/5	0/13	3(1+2)/20	0/17	0/22
Collective worship	6(0+6)/14	0/6	2(0+2)/13	8(0+8)/24	5(2+3)/22	9(2+7)/34
Higher education						
Staff	7(1+6)/14	0/5	2(0+2)/6	8(0+8)/16	4(0+4)/10	14(1+13)/32
Students	7(1+6)/14	0/5	2(0+2)/5	8(0+8)/15	4(1+3)/11	16(1+15)/33
Policies	3(1+2)/12	0/5	0/5	3(1+2)/16	0/8	4(2+2)/29
Practices	2(1+1)/12	0/5	2(0+2)/5	3(1+2)/16	0/9	7(2+5)/29
Local education authorities						
Officials	3(0+3)/12	0/5	1(0+1)/15	1(0+1)/19	0(0+1)/14	8(2+6)/28
Policies	4(1+3)/14	1(0+1)/6	3(0+3)/16	4(0+4)/21	3(1+2)/15	5(3+2)/28
Practices	3(1+2)/13	1(0+1)/6	3(0+3)/16	4(0+4)/20	4(1+3)/17	6(3+3)/29
Private sector employers						
Managers	4(1+3)/16	1(0+1)/5	2(0+2)/11	8(1+7)/20	6(1+5)/18	24(3+21)/42
Colleagues	5(1+4)/18	1(0+1)/5	3(0+3)/11	10(1+9)/22	6(0+6)/18	24(2+22)/41
Policies	3(0+3)/15	2(0+2)/6	1(0+1)/10	3(1+2)/20	3(1+2)/18	7(2+5)/38
Practices	3(0+3)/14	2(0+2)/6	0/10	3(1+2)/20	4(2+2)/18	9(2+7)/37

Public sector employers						
Managers	4(1+3)/17	1(0+1)/5	0/11	4(0+4)/18	5(0+5)/19	21(2+19)/36
Colleagues	3(1+2)/16	1(0+1)/5	2(0+2)/11	7(1+6)/20	5(0+5)/19	21(1+20)/35
Policies	2(0+2)/14	2(0+2)/6	0/11	2(0+2)/20	2(0+2)/18	7(2+5)/34
Practices	2(0+2)/15	2(0+2)/6	2(0+2)/11	5(0+5)/20	3(1+2)/19	8(2+6)/33
Voluntary sector employers						
Managers	1(1+0)/15	0/4	1(0+1)/12	0/19	2(0+2)/16	7(1+6)/28
Colleagues	4(1+3)/17	0/4	2(0+2)/12	2(0+2)/20	2(0+2)/16	7(1+6)/27
Policies	1(0+1)/14	0/4	0/11	0/19	0/16	4(1+3)/27
Practices	2(0+2)/14	0/4	0/11	1(0+1)/17	0/16	5(1+4)/27
Jobcentres						
Staff	2(0+2)/16	1(0+1)/5	0/10	1(0+1)/18	2(0+2)/9	2(0+2)/31
Policies	0/14	0/5	0/10	1(0+1)/17	0/8	1(0+1)/30
Practices	0/14	0/5	0/10	1(0+1)/18	1(0+1)/9	1(1+0)/30
Private employment agencies						
Staff	2(0+2)/14	0/4	0/10	1(0+1)/15	1(0+1)/7	4(0+4)/29
Policies	1(0+1)/14	0/4	0/10	1(1+0)/15	0/7	1(0+1)/28
Practices	1(0+1)/14	0/4	0/10	1(1+0)/15	1(0+1)/8	1(0+1)/27
Owning or buying a house						
Estate agent staff	2(0+2)/16	0/6	0/12	0/20	1(0+1)/19	2(0+2)/37
Policies/practices	1(0+1)/16	0/6	0/10	0/19	0/18	2(0+2)/38
Neighbours	3(0+3)/18	0/6	2(0+2)/13	1(0+1)/21	4(0+4)/20	15(0+15)/39
Private renting						
Landlords	2(0+2)/15	0/6	0/10	0/20	1(0+1)/19	7(0+7)/39
Policies/practices	2(0+2)/16	0/6	0/10	0/20	1(0+1)/19	3(0+3)/36
Lettings agents	0/14	0/6	0/9	0/19	0/19	4(0+4)/35
Policies/practices	0/14	0/6	0/9	0/19	0/19	1(0+1)/33
Other tenants	2(0+2)/14	0/6	0/9	0/20	4(0+4)/18	7(0+7)/36

	Pentecostal	Presbyterian	Roman Catholic	Independent	Ecumenical	Other
Renting from a council						
Council staff	2(0+2)/15	0/6	0/13	0/18	0/17	3(0+3)/33
Policies	2(1+1)/16	0/6	0/11	0/17	0/17	0/32
Practices	2(1+1)/16	0/6	0/11	0/18	0/17	1(0+1)/31
Other tenants	3(0+3)/15	1(0+1)/6	0/10	0/18	4(0+4)/17	8(0+8)/33
Tenants' associations	0/14	0/5	0/10	0/17	1(0+1)/16	2(0+2)/29
Renting from housing associations						
HA staff	0/15	0/5	0/9	0/17	1(0+1)/14	2(0+2)/30
Policies	0/14	0/5	0/10	0/17	0/14	1(0+1)/30
Practices	1(0+1)/14	0/5	0/9	0/17	0/14	2(0+2)/30
Other tenants	1(0+1)/14	0/5	0/9	0/17	3(0+3)/13	6(0+6)/30
Tenants' associations	0/13	0/5	0/9	0/17	0/12	2(0+2)/29
Surgeries and health centres						
GPs/medical staff	0/15	1(1+0)/5	1(0+1)/15	1(0+1)/23	2(0+2)/20	21(1+20)/46
Non-medical staff	0/15	1(1+0)/5	1(0+1)/15	0/23	2(0+2)/20	15(1+14)/44
Policies/practices	1(1+0)/17	1(1+0)/5	2(0+2)/15	0/22	1(0+1)/21	10(0+10)/45
NHS hospitals						
Medical staff	1(0+1)/16	1(1+0)/5	1(0+1)/15	0/23	2(0+2)/20	17(2+15)/44
Non-medical staff	0/15	1(1+0)/5	1(0+1)/13	0/23	1(0+1)/20	11(1+10)/44
Patients	2(0+2)/16	1(1+0)/5	0/13	0/23	3(0+3)/20	9(0+9)/41
Policies	1(1+0)/16	1(1+0)/5	1(0+1)/13	0/23	0/21	6(0+6)/37
Practices	1(1+0)/16	1(1+0)/5	1(0+1)/12	0/23	0/21	8(1+7)/37
Private health care						
Medical staff	0/12	1(1+0)/5	1(0+1)/11	0/22	0/14	6(0+6)/30
Non-medical staff	0/12	1(1+0)/5	1(0+1)/11	0/22	0/14	5(0+5)/30
Patients	0/12	1(1+0)/5	0/11	0/22	0/14	4(0+4)/29
Policies/practices	0/12	1(1+0)/5	0/11	0/22	0/14	2(0+2)/29

The police service						
Police officers	4(0+4)/16	1(1+0)/5	1(0+1)/14	2(0+2)/21	3(0+3)/20	9(0+9)/38
Policies	1(0+1)/14	1(1+0)/5	0/12	1(0+1)/21	0/19	3(0+3)/34
Practices	1(0+1)/14	1(1+0)/5	0/11	3(0+3)/21	2(0+2)/20	6(0+6)/35
Legal services						
Lawyers	0/13	1(0+1)/5	0/12	0/20	0/17	7(0+7)/34
Court staff	0/13	1(0+1)/5	0/9	1(0+1)/20	0/14	6(0+6)/28
Policies/practices	1(0+1)/12	1(0+1)/5	0/8	1(0+1)/20	0/15	7(0+7)/28
The prison service						
Prison staff	2(0+2)/11	1(0+1)/3	3(0+3)/6	0/18	2(0+2)/10	2(0+2)/16
Inmates	2(0+2)/11	1(0+1)/3	0/4	0/16	2(0+2)/9	3(0+3)/15
Policies	0/10	1(0+1)/3	1(0+1)/5	0/16	0/9	1(0+1)/14
Practices	0/10	1(0+1)/3	1(0+1)/5	0/16	0/10	2(0+2)/15
The probation service						
Staff	0/9	1(0+1)/3	0/5	0/19	1(0+1)/12	3(1+2)/13
Policies	0/8	1(0+1)/3	0/5	0/17	0/12	1(1+0)/12
Practices	0/8	0/3	0/5	0/18	1(0+1)/12	2(1+1)/12
Immigration authorities						
Staff	1(0+1)/7	0/4	1(0+1)/5	0/17	2(0+2)/8	5(3+2)/16
Policies	0/6	0/4	1(0+1)/5	0/16	0/7	5(3+2)/17
Practices	0/6	0/4	1(0+1)/6	0/16	0/7	5(3+2)/16
Social services						
Staff	6(3+3)/15	3(0+3)/5	1(0+1)/15	2(1+1)/24	3(0+3)/22	14(5+9)/33
Policies	3(3+0)/14	2(0+2)/5	0/12	2(1+1)/24	0/21	10(3+7)/31
Practices	4(3+1)/14	3(0+3)/5	0/13	1(1+0)/24	2(0+2)/21	11(5+6)/31
The Benefits Agency						
Staff	0/11	0/5	0/13	0/24	3(0+3)/18	2(1+1)/32
Policies/practices	0/11	0/5	0/12	0/24	1(0+1)/17	2(1+1)/32

	Pentecostal	Presbyterian	Roman Catholic	Independent	Ecumenical	Other
Local authority planning services						
Planners	5(1+4)/13	0/5	0/12	1(0+1)/20	2(1+1)/18	15(3+12)/33
Policies	3(1+2)/12	1(0+1)/5	0/11	2(0+2)/20	0/17	8(0+8)/30
Practices	4(1+3)/12	1(0+1)/5	0/11	3(1+2)/20	3(1+2)/18	11(3+8)/32
Local authority leisure services						
Staff	1(0+1)/13	0/5	0/11	2(0+2)/23	2(0+2)/19	0/31
Policies	0/13	0/5	0/10	0/22	1(0+1)/18	0/30
Practices	1(0+1)/14	0/5	0/10	1(0+1)/23	1(0+1)/18	0/30
Public transport						
Staff	0/14	0/5	1(0+1)/14	0/22	3(0+3)/21	0/35
Policies/practices	2(0+2)/13	0/5	1(0+1)/12	0/22	2(0+2)/19	0/34
Shops and stores						
Staff	3(0+3)/17	0/5	1(0+1)/16	1(0+1)/23	1(0+1)/21	1(0+1)/36
Customers	0/15	1(0+1)/5	1(0+1)/16	0/23	5(1+4)/20	1(0+1)/36
Policies/practices	1(1+0)/15	1(1+0)/5	2(0+2)/16	2(1+1)/23	1(0+1)/18	1(0+1)/36
Charities and trusts						
Staff	1(0+1)/12	0/2	2(0+2)/13	1(0+1)/19	2(0+2)/19	4(1+3)/22
Policies	2(1+1)/10	0/3	2(0+2)/12	1(0+1)/19	3(1+2)/18	4(1+3)/22
Practices	4(1+3)/10	0/3	2(0+2)/12	1(0+1)/19	3(1+2)/19	4(2+2)/22
Local government funding						
Staff	3(1+2)/12	0/3	1(0+1)/13	2(0+2)/16	5(0+5)/17	1(1+0)/13
Policies	3(1+2)/9	1(0+1)/4	0/11	3(0+3)/16	3(1+2)/16	1(1+0)/12
Practices	3(1+2)/9	1(0+1)/4	2(0+2)/12	2(0+2)/16	5(1+4)/18	1(1+0)/12
Central government funding						
Staff	1(0+1)/6	0/3	0/11	3(0+3)/12	2(0+2)/9	3(2+1)/13
Policies	2(1+1)/6	1(0+1)/4	1(0+1)/12	4(1+3)/13	2(1+1)/9	2(1+1)/12
Practices	3(1+2)/6	1(0+1)/4	1(0+1)/12	3(0+3)/12	3(1+2)/9	2(1+1)/12

Public donation

General public	1(1+0)/10	0/3	6(0+6)/14	0/16	2(0+2)/20	7(2+5)/21
National newspapers/magazines						
Journalists	10(4+6)/16	2(0+2)/3	13(2+11)/15	15(4+11)/23	13(4+9)/21	41(16+25)/46
Coverage of org.	5(2+3)/14	2(1+1)/4	9(1+8)/13	10(1+9)/20	6(1+5)/16	43(15+28)/50
Coverage of religion	12(4+8)/19	2(1+1)/4	13(2+11)/16	17(5+12)/24	14(4+10)/23	45(18+27)/50
Local newspapers/magazines						
Journalists	7(1+6)/20	3(1+2)/5	8(1+7)/13	10(0+10)/24	6(1+5)/20	38(9+29)/48
Coverage of org.	5(1+4)/17	3(1+2)/5	4(1+3)/10	5(0+5)/22	4(1+3)/20	35(9+26)/45
Coverage of religion	6(3+3)/16	1(1+0)/4	7(1+6)/12	8(0+8)/23	5(1+4)/21	39(10+29)/49
National radio						
Journalists	9(3+6)/13	3(1+2)/5	8(1+7)/12	12(3+9)/23	8(2+6)/18	33(10+23)/41
Coverage of org.	5(2+3)/10	2(1+1)/5	5(0+5)/8	5(1+4)/14	6(1+5)/14	34(9+25)/42
Coverage of religion	9(3+6)/14	2(1+1)/5	9(1+8)/12	10(3+7)/21	10(2+8)/19	34(11+23)/41
Local radio						
Journalists	7(1+6)/17	2(1+1)/5	5(0+5)/13	8(1+7)/22	3(0+3)/19	27(2+25)/40
Coverage of org.	4(1+3)/15	3(1+2)/5	4(0+4)/10	5(0+5)/18	2(0+2)/17	26(2+24)/38
Coverage of religion	6(2+4)/15	1(1+0)/4	6(0+6)/13	7(0+7)/21	3(0+3)/18	27(4+23)/39
Television						
Journalists	10(3+7)/14	3(1+2)/5	11(2+9)/13	12(8+4)/22	9(3+6)/19	38(12+26)/46
Coverage of org.	7(2+5)/15	2(1+1)/5	6(1+5)/9	5(2+3)/16	6(1+5)/13	38(12+26)/45
Coverage of religion	13(6+7)/18	2(1+1)/5	10(3+7)/13	14(6+8)/21	13(4+9)/21	40(13+27)/46

Part 3

Measures that should be considered in order to combat unfair treatment on the basis of religion*

	Bahá'í	Buddhist	Christian	Hindu	Jain	Jewish	Muslim	NRM/ Pagan	Sikh	Zoroas- trian	Inter- faith
No new action	0	1	18	0	0	1	2	0	2	0	0
More teaching of comparative religion in schools	22	28	128	33	6	30	47	20	29	6	15
Policy reviews to promote equal treatment	11	7	115	16	3	9	40	11	24	6	9
Better training of staff/employees	9	11	153	26	6	22	41	8	21	5	13
Public education programmes	23	22	159	20	2	25	45	20	20	5	13
Voluntary codes of practice	3	1	91	10	1	9	17	1	9	4	4
Changes in the law/introduce new law	5	7	63	18	1	9	49	12	17	1	7
Other	0	1	15	1	0	3	5	1	0	0	1
Total	24	30	286	35	6	36	67	24	34	6	22

* Respondents were asked to choose up to 3 options – see explanatory notes

Glossary

Bahá'í faith

Founded in Iran in the mid-19th century, the Bahá'í faith places great emphasis on the unity of all religions and on the unity of humanity. Bahá'ís believe that the founders of the world's great religions have been messengers and manifestations of God, bringing progressive revelation of the one God and one religion to humankind at different times and in different places. Every Bahá'í is under a spiritual obligation to pray daily, practice monogamy and abstain totally from narcotics and alcohol. There are approximately 6,000 living in the UK, most of whom are converts.

Diwali

The Hindu festival which marks the beginning of the New Year. It is the celebration of light over darkness and knowledge over ignorance. Lamps are lit to illuminate the Goddess Lakshmi's way to the home and to celebrate the return of Lord Rama and his wife Sita to Rama's kingdom after 14 years of exile. Sikhs also celebrate Diwali, but for different reasons.

Eid

Eid al-Fitr is the Muslim festival which celebrates the breaking of the month-long Ramadan fast. Around one to two days are taken to celebrate, presents are exchanged and donations given to charity. The celebration emphasises unity and togetherness.

Five Ks

This is part of the strict dress code for practising Khalsa (or initiated) Sikhs. It is called the 5 Ks as the Punjabi word for each begins with the sound of "K."

  Kesh (uncut hair and beard)
  Kangha (a small wooden comb)
  Kachha (a special undergarment)
  Kara (a metal bracelet)
  Kirpan (a ceremonial sword or dagger)

Grail Church

The Apostolic Church of the Holy Grail is a revival of the early Celtic Church that existed in Britain before the arrival of St Augustine. There are other versions of Grail Christianity with links to the New Age movement. It is believed by followers that the original British Church was founded by Jesus Christ at Glastonbury and developed by Joseph of Arimathea, who brought the Holy Grail to England.

Gurdwara
Members of the Sikh religion congregate at this place of worship. It is also a centre for religious education and social and welfare activities. Shoes must be removed and heads covered as a mark of respect. Alcohol and tobacco are forbidden on the premises.

Hijab
This is the headscarf worn by many Muslim women.

Inter-faith
This refers to arrangements whereby people of different faiths come together to share views or work together on particular projects. It does not necessarily imply a search for unity, but it does convey more than 'multi-faith' (which often refers to a way of organising on a religiously inclusive basis that can be found among secular organisations).

Jainism
Along with Hinduism and Buddhism, this is one of the three ancient religious traditions of India. There is a strong belief in non-violence and the avoidance of all physical or even mental harm to any living being. It is estimated that some 25,000 to 30,000 Jains live in the UK.

Kirpan
One of the Five Ks (see above) in the Sikh dress code, the kirpan is a ceremonial sword or dagger which represents dignity and self-respect and protection of the weak.

Kunti-Mala
These are beads worn around the neck that are believed to provide protection at the time of death.

Madrassah
Literally meaning "a place of study", this term is generally used in the UK to refer to Qur'anic schools for children.

Mezuzah
A small box containing words from scripture written on a piece of parchment, which is fixed to door posts in synagogues and many Jewish homes. It signifies the sanctity of home and communal life.

Mormonism
Founded by Joseph Smith in about 1830, Mormons believe in the Second Coming of Jesus Christ and in the need for the restoration of the true church. The largest group is the Church of Jesus Christ of Latter-day Saints, which has its headquarters in Salt Lake City. *The Book of Mormon*, which is said to have been revealed to Smith, is used alongside the Bible. There is a strong emphasis on the family and on missionary work.

New Church
Also known as the House Church movement, this term is used for evangelical groups who see themselves as restoring a more authentic form of Christianity and often meet in private homes or hired public premises rather than in traditional church buildings.

New Religious Movements (NRM)
A general term for a wide variety of movements, most of which have developed in their present form since the Second World War. There is no general agreement about the precise definition, but examples of movements that are often included are Unificationists, the Hare Krishna movement, the Church of Scientology, Neo-paganism, a variety of New Age beliefs and a number of organisations that are often popularly described as 'cults'.

Paganism
There are several spiritual movements within Paganism, some of which are an attempt to revive the ancient polytheistic beliefs of Europe and the Middle East. There is typically a concern with ecology and the cyclical patterns of nature, and often a belief in magic and witchcraft. Paganism should be distinguished from Satanism.

Pentecostalism
A charismatic and fundamentalist Christian movement characterised by the belief in a post-conversion religious experience (corresponding to the descent of the Holy Spirit on the 12 disciples on the day of Pentecost). Someone who has undergone this 'baptism in the Spirit' has the gift of speaking in tongues and may also be able to prophesy or to heal. Pentecostalists believe in the primacy of the scriptures. The movement includes a significant number of black-majority churches.

Sai Baba
A spiritual organisation founded by Sathya Sai Baba, which includes people of all faiths. Sai Baba teaches that the divinity in human nature will be realised through leading a moral life, rendering selfless service to others in need and developing love and respect for all life. There are over 145 centres and groups in the UK.

Unificationist

The Unification Movement was founded in South Korea in 1954 by Sun Myung Moon (hence the popular epithet 'Moonies'). The movement believes that the restoration of divine rule on earth was inaugurated by Jesus Christ, but that the union of Moon and his wife (known as 'The True Parents') is necessary for its completion. Members or followers currently organise in a variety of ways and the movement includes businesses as well as religious organisations. Many are incorporated in the Family Federation for World Peace and Unification.

Vihara

The place of residence of Buddhist monks.

Zoroastrianism

This is the ancient, pre-Islamic religion of Iran. British Zoroastrians are either of (Indian) Parsi descent or Iranian Zoroastrians who trace their ancestry back to the ancient Persians. The religion was founded by the prophet and reformer Zoroaster (Zarathushtra), who proclaimed the worship of Ahura Mazda (the Wise Lord). There is a long-established community of around 5-10,000 Zoroastrians in the UK. The first three Asian MPs were of Parsi origin, the first being elected in 1892.

RDS Publications

Requests for Publications

Copies of our publications and a list of those currently available may be obtained from:

> Home Office
> Research, Development and Statistics Directorate
> Communications Development Unit
> Room 201, Home Office
> 50 Queen Anne's Gate
> London SW1H 9AT
> Telephone: 020 7273 2084 (answerphone outside of office hours)
> Facsimile: 020 7222 0211
> E-mail: publications.rds@homeoffice.gsi.gov.uk

alternatively

why not visit the RDS website at
> Internet: http://www.homeoffice.gov.uk/rds/index.html

where many of our publications are available to be read on screen or downloaded for printing.